Frank Stewart, a full-time professional bridge teacher, player, and writer, is a Life Master of the American Contract Bridge League and a winner of more than forty tournament events. He is a Contributing Editor for the ACBL *Bulletin,* and his articles have also appeared in *Bridge World* and *Popular Bridge* magazines.

BETTER BRIDGE

for the Advancing Player

AN INTRODUCTION TO CONSTRUCTIVE THINKING AT THE BRIDGE TABLE

FRANK STEWART

A SPECTRUM BOOK

Prentice-Hall, Inc., Englewood Cliffs, New Jersey 07632

Library of Congress Cataloging in Publication Data

Stewart, Frank, 1946 Oct. 16-
   Better bridge for the advancing player.

   "A Spectrum Book"
   Includes index.
   1. Contract bridge. I. Title
  GV1282.3.S6647   1984   795.41'53   83-17719
  ISBN 0-13-071951-X
  ISBN 0-13-071944-7 (pbk.)

This book is available at a special discount when ordered in bulk quantities.
Contact Prentice-Hall, Inc., General Publishing Division, Special Sales,
Englewood Cliffs, N. J. 07632.

10 9 8 7 6 5 4 3 2

Printed in the United States of America

ISBN 0-13-071951-X

ISBN 0-13-071944-7 {PBK.}

Prentice-Hall International, Inc., *London*
Prentice-Hall of Australia Pty. Limited, *Sydney*
Prentice-Hall of Canada Inc., *Toronto*
Prentice-Hall of India Private Limited, *New Delhi*
Prentice-Hall of Japan, Inc., *Tokyo*
Prentice-Hall of Southeast Asia Pte. Ltd., *Singapore*
Whitehall Books Limited, *Wellington, New Zealand*
Editora Prentice-Hall do Brasil Ltda., *Rio de Janeiro*

To Char

doesn't play bridge,
still the bestest wife

Contents

Foreword

Most bridge enthusiasts aren't willing to improve their games at the expense of drudgery. And many bridge books, written by experts qualified on the subject matter but lacking the necessary literary talent, end up collecting dust. I promise you this book will be an exception.

As my occasional partner, more frequent opponent, and constant friend, Frank Stewart has the technical bridge knowledge to write a first-rate book. He has been a successful bridge teacher and lecturer for several years in Birmingham, Alabama, known for his emphasis on orderly and logical thought in solving problems at the bridge table. What was gratifying to me and held me spellbound was the realization from the offset that he also possesses the very rare talent for communicating in such a way that his material is always interesting.

The bridge student who wishes to learn just how the expert thought processes evolve has the unique opportunity to examine closely just why the expert bids and plays as he does. In each of the 90 hands there are multiple lessons—not obscure, but applicable to everyday encounters at the bridge table. For the light reader, there are descriptions of games from the world of bridge, ranging from rubber bridge at Grandma's house to pressure-packed situations at the world's most prestigious tournaments.

Frank Stewart has arrived as a significant bridge author. He is ready to achieve great heights in his field. I'm already looking foward to his next book. After you finish this one, you will be, too.

Thomas K. Sanders

(Author's Note: Tom Sanders, one of the most respected men and feared competitors in the world of tournament bridge, is a member of the National Board of Directors of the American Contract Bridge League; a many-times National Champion; and Non-playing Captain of the 1981 United States International Team that captured the Bermuda Bowl, the symbol of the World Championship of bridge. Thanks, Tom.)

Preface

This book is written for you, the player who is becoming captivated by contract bridge. Perhaps you've played enough to see that there is no more stimulating mental challenge to be found in any game. And you want to learn more about it. You want to improve, to get more from the time you spend at the bridge table. And, of course, you want to be a winner, to be looked up to as the master of a complex game. Bridge is an ego trip for all of us who play it.

I have assumed you to be well past the stage of the wide eyed beginner, and so I have tried to minimize the presentation of a lot of musty rules in the text, and concentrate instead on thought processes and the type of thinking on which some of those rules are based. After all, you know that nobody can play and enjoy this game by blindly following any set of rules. The appeal of the game lies in the almost infinite variety of problem situations the players may face. This is definitely a *thinking* person's game, and learning *how to think* is important.

Each of the hands offers problems to be solved in both the auction and the declarer play. My aim has been to show something of how the successful player thinks in attempting to solve these problems. Clear thinking is the most important attribute of the winning player, and the idea is that if you are exposed to lots of the right type of thinking, maybe some of it will rub off on you.

In the play problems, the emphasis is repeatedly on drawing inferences from the opponents' bidding and play, as well as on generally good technique. In the auction, the discussion is mainly on hand evaluation, competitive judgment, and a sound knowledge of the fundamentals of good bidding. In the back of the text, you will find an index in which specific topics are listed, as well as a glossary of terms, in case the world of tournament bridge is foreign to you.

To make things (hopefully) more readable, I have inserted each problem into a real life setting from the world of bridge. Almost all the hands are from actual play anyhow. Very few have been constructed just to illustrate a point. In places, I'm afraid I have allowed my opinions about certain aspects of bridge today to creep into the commentary, and for that I have to ask your indulgence, even if you don't agree with some of my quaint views. My purpose is not really to mount a soap box, but only to provide a diversion within the course of the instruction.

The first set of hands is not especially difficult, and will serve, perhaps, as a warm up or review. The later ones are tougher. In any case, when a question is posed (and followed by centered boxes ■ ■ ■), you are advised to try to think out some sort of answer before proceeding further. If you do so, the book will be most useful as a self teacher.

Frank Stewart

Acknowledgments

Many of the hands in this book are from my own experience. I muffed quite a few of them, in fact, and perhaps that is why they have stayed in my memory. A few are adapted from various sources, or fabricated outright. In addition, I am indebted to experts Steve Beatty, Mike Cappelletti, and Paul Munafo, each of whom supplied me with a good hand.

Many thanks go to: Henry Francis and Sue Emery, at the ACBL *Bulletin;* Edgar Kaplan and Jeff Rubens of *The Bridge World* magazine; and Robert Wolenik of *Popular Bridge* magazine; for their kind permissions to borrow back some hands from various articles of mine that appeared in their fine publications.

Special thanks are due my friend and frequent partner, Dr. Ralph Z. Levene, without whose gracious and valuable assistance I could not have produced this work.

part one

NOT SO HARD

You arrived at the tournament the night before the main events began, determined to manage a good night's sleep. Trying to play tough bridge when you are worn out after a drive of several hours is murder, or, at least, that's what you kept telling yourself. So naturally, you were inveigled into playing in the Kickoff Game. This is a not too serious event. I played in one at a Regional held over the Thanksgiving weekend once, and first prize was a live turkey. The bird, gobbling away in his crate, was duly presented to the winners at the start of the afternoon session the next day. There were, needless to say, a lot of side-splitting comments offered by some of the other players at this spectacle. More often, the prize in a game like this is something less whimsical, like free entry to the rest of the tournament. At any rate, the Kickoff Game gives people who want it a chance to tune up for the bigger doings the next day.

Pretty soon, you pick up this hand:

♠ K108652
♥ 63
♦ AK
♣ QJ3

Neither side is vulnerable, and you happily open ONE SPADE. LHO (left hand opponent, for the uninitiated) overcalls TWO HEARTS and partner raises you to TWO SPADES. RHO now comes in with THREE DIAMONDS. What should you do?

■   ■   ■

This isn't a very close decision. You should feel like competing. You have no heart wasteage underneath the two heart bidder, no "slow" diamond tricks behind the three diamond bidder (the Ace and King of diamonds will be useful cards for you if you are declarer; something like the Q10x of diamonds would be worthless for offense). Most important, you have a sixth spade, and that alone is enough to suggest that you bid further. In these part-score situations, when your side has a reasonable fit and a reasonable share of the high cards, you frequently want to compete to the *three* level, unless you can see some good reason not to. (If you had one less spade, for instance, your *shaky trump holding* would be reason enough to *pass* three diamonds around to partner. See also hand #49.)

If you bid three spades here, will partner think you are inviting game? No, a three spade bid is strictly competitive in this sequence. Partner should forget about bidding four unless he or she has a very unusual raise. If you thought there was a chance for game, you could bid three *hearts* as a game try, or just take the pressure off by shooting out a game bid yourself.

All pass to your THREE SPADES. The opening lead is the club Ace, and the dummy is seen to have a good hand:

♠ QJ3
♡ AQ103
◇ 73
♣ 9642
□
♠ K108652
♡ 63
◇ AK
♣ QJ3

Partner must have been sorely tempted to go ahead and bid four spades, but discipline prevailed. His raise to two spades is also worthy of note. Some players might have hammered the two heart overcall instead, but it is a well known principle that you should not go "headhunting" and double the opposition before you show a fit, if you have one, for partner. If they had been vulnerable, a double would perhaps have stood to gain more. (A one-trick set would be worth 200 points and a top score if no game was makable with your cards.)

After winning the first trick, LHO continues with the King and another club, and RHO ruffs the third round. It begins to look like you made a good stop. A diamond is returned to your Ace. You lead a trump to the Queen and RHO's Ace, take the diamond return, and draw the last trump. Now, is there anything more to this hand than to finesse in hearts?

■   ■   ■

The heart finesse is a heavy bet to succeed when LHO bid the suit, sure. But there is no point in taking any chances. You run the rest of your spades, and the end position is:

♠ —
♡ AQ
♢ —
♣ 9
□
♠ 5
♡ 63
♢ —
♣ —

When you lead the last of your trumps, LHO has to come down to two cards, and one of them must be the club ten, since dummy's club remains as a threat. You discard the club from dummy and lead a heart. LHO plays the Jack. You know that his other card is the high club, so you go up with the heart *Ace* and drop the singleton King offside. LHO's hand was:

♠ x
♡ J9xxxx
♢ Qx
♣ AK10x

A heart shift at trick two would have given you a very tough guess. The line of play you used is known as a "show-up squeeze." The position is a very common one, and by playing the hand this way, you can take yourself off any guess in the end-game. Incidentally, even if the only thing you know about squeezes is how to make fresh orange juice, it is always a good idea to *run off all your winners* when you are in the position of having all the tricks but one. Even if your opponents aren't legitimately squeezed, they might make a discarding error under the pressure of your long suit. There are, after all, more turkeys around than prizes for the Kickoff Pairs.

2

The other day, feeling in a magnanimous mood, you decided you would drop in on your grandmother and brighten up her day a little. Of course, there was a hot bridge game in progress at Grandma's when you arrived. Four of the sweetest looking little old ladies (LOLs) you ever saw. You were quickly invited to join the game, and of course, you graciously consented. Grandma has told all her friends what a fine bridge player one of her grandchildren is, and you wouldn't want to let her down, now would you?

This is the first hand of the game. As dealer, you hold:

♠ AK10953
♡ A104
♢ 65
♣ 82

You open ONE SPADE. This may send shock waves through the air at Grandma's house and it may not. Some LOLs are confirmed point counters who quail at the very thought of opening the bidding with a shred less than thirteen solid high card points. Then there are others who were trained in the Culbertsonian honor-trick method of hand evaluation and have an inkling that, even in the Gorenian day and age, an Ace might possibly be worth more than two Queens. Really, this hand lacks nothing for an opening bid. You have some potential tricks (that's the bottom line), good defense, and an easy second bid. What more could you ask for? So you're short a couple of Jacks. Big deal.

Partner murmurs a quiet TWO DIAMONDS and you rebid TWO SPADES. FOUR SPADES from across the table. All pass.

LHO leads the club five, and a suitable dummy comes down:

♠ QJ2
♡ 652
◇ A9742
♣ AQ

□

♠ AK10953
♡ A104
◇ 65
♣ 82

Plan the play.

■   ■   ■

Being a careful player, you begin by *counting your sure winners* and find that you have nine of them and must develop one more. There are two possibilities: the club finesse may work; or, you could try to set up dummy's diamonds. It would be nice if you could try *both* chances, but if you take a losing club hook at trick one, the little old ladies will surely switch to hearts ("*Through strength, up to weakness*"). And they will have to make four tricks; a club, two hearts, and a diamond. So it looks like you must decide right away whether to stake your contract on the club finesse, or give up on that chance and go after diamonds.

■   ■   ■

Let's see. The club finesse is a 50-50 proposition. Maybe less, with a little old lady on your left. Some LOLs would rather meet up with a mad rapist in a dark alley than lead away from a King under any circumstances. How about the diamond play? You can set up a long card there if diamonds are no worse than 4-2 (provided trumps are not 4-0). You have three entries to dummy with the two high spades and the diamond Ace, so you can ruff two diamonds if necessary, then get back to cash your established winner. The odds in your favor (you may have to take my word for this) are about 75 percent.

So, you go right up with the club Ace and plan to rely on diamonds. To begin with, you cannot draw trumps. Your transportation would disappear. You must go after your side suit immediately. Also, you must *duck* the first diamond. If you play Ace and another, you will have used up one of your entries before any diamonds have been ruffed and you might come up an entry short.

The opponents will win the diamond, cash their King of clubs, and shift to a heart. You win, play a diamond to the Ace, and ruff a diamond *high*. If diamonds split 3-3, draw three rounds of trumps ending in dummy and take your good diamonds, discarding your heart losers. If, as is more likely, there is still a high diamond out against you after three rounds of the suit, return to dummy with a spade honor and ruff another diamond high. The fifth diamond will be good now, and you can cross over in trumps to cash it.

The little old ladies in the Tuesday afternoon game at Grandma's will doubtless be impressed and Grandma will beam with ill concealed pride. Maybe she'll even bake you a chocolate cake or something.

3

You went off to play in a Sectional only three hundred miles or so down the road. During one of the Pair games, you found yourself opposed by a young man of about twelve, playing with somebody who looked like his mother. It was nice to find a young person taking an interest in the game. Bridge just has to be a great game for kids, since it teaches many virtues that are worthwhile to the young: discipline, partnership cooperation, modesty, generosity, ethics, self control, logical thinking, and a host of others. Of course, there are fewer prodigies at bridge than there may be in chess, where Fischer won the U.S. Championship at the age of thirteen. Bridge is somewhat less of an intuitive game, and experience and maturity count a great deal.

For most teenagers, who lack the late developing trait of patience, the problem is to keep them interested in the game long enough for them to learn to love it. But every now and then, you see a young player in the adult world of tournament bridge. I think maybe there will be more soon. Stamina is an important factor in tournament bridge, and the young have energy to burn and intense powers of concentration. Incidentally, the youngest Life Master in history achieved that rank at age 11, the record having been lowered regularly of late.

On the first board of the round against "The Kid," you face a problem situation:

♠ KQ104
♡ J1053
◇ AK63
♣ Q

4-4-4-1 hands are about the most awkward ones to describe. Trying to get all your suits into the bidding, locate a fit if there is one, and keep from getting overboard in the process can be a real headache. There is disagreement, even among experts, on how you should begin to describe these hands. *Very strong* hands with the 4-4-4-1 pattern are especially troublesome. You may not be willing to open two clubs (artificial) because that would lose you a round of bidding that you need to find a suit. Even if you can open a strong, natural two bid, partner may assume your suit is stronger, or longer than just four cards. But if you open just one of a suit, it may go all pass when you can make a *slam* in some other suit! Handling these hands is one of the weaker areas of Standard American, and some other bidding systems have reserved a two club or two diamond opening(!) specifically to cope with them.

You can open one diamond on the hand above, but you will have to worry about what you will do if partner responds one notrump or two clubs. The trouble with a one spade opening is that you would have to guess which of your red suits to show if partner responded one notrump or two clubs. Also, partner might raise a one spade opening to two with three spades and five hearts. (But, spades might be raised, allowing you to reach a lucrative 4-3 fit.) As for a one heart opening, that would appeal to very few players because of the weak suit. Which opening do you choose?

■   ■   ■

After thinking it over, you decide to open ONE DIAMOND. You are willing to rebid two notrump over two clubs or pass a one notrump response with your singleton club *honor*, which should make the play a little more tenable in notrump. Passing one notrump with your stiff club wouldn't be so outrageous. Partner should have at least four clubs on the bidding. He didn't bid a major suit or raise your diamonds, after all.

But over your one diamond, partner pleasantly raises to THREE DIAMONDS, forcing as you play. You try THREE SPADES to show where your side strength lies and partner surprises you with a raise to FOUR SPADES. He's unlikely to have four spades since he failed to respond one spade initially, but perhaps you can handle the play in a robust 4-3 fit. This is matchpoints, remember, and the major suit game will score more points than five diamonds.

"The Kid" leads the club Ace, and dummy is about as expected:

♠ AJ7
♡ A7
◇ QJ942
♣ 853

□

♠ KQ104
♡ J1053
◇ AK63
♣ Q

The opponents, as you fear, continue clubs after winning the first trick, and you have to worry about going out of control. We will see that declarer has various counters available against a *forcing* defense; but here, you have side tricks to cash, and so you must try to *draw* all the trumps so that you can safely cash them. How can you handle the play?

■   ■   ■

A simple *loser-on-loser* play will come to your aid here. Perhaps we should say "losers-on-losers" in this case. Discard hearts on the second and third rounds of clubs. After that, *dummy* will be out of clubs. You can ruff any further club leads on the table and preserve the four trumps in your hand to draw trumps with. Your last heart will go on dummy's fifth diamond, and you will make ten tricks unless the trumps split horrendously. This might be worth a fair score to you, since a diamond contract may be held to five, and there is always somebody in three notrump on hands like this.

You *need* to get a good score on this board, incidentally, because on the next one, "The Kid" is going to roar into an enthusiastic six spades against you, exercising the ebullience of youth. The contract will roll home, too, even though it takes a couple of finesses and a 3-3 split in trumps. Youth will be served, they say.

4

In his classic *Five Weeks to Winning Bridge,* Alfred Shienwold wryly and accurately observed that the true worth of a bridge hand may depend on extraneous factors, such as your partner's skill as declarer, who in the game is discouraged, who has had too much to drink, and so on. Shienwold was trying to point out that hand evaluation is a tricky business, with few hard and fast rules that are cherished as the gospel truth. The worth of an Ace, for instance, can change somewhat according to the circumstances. To a beginner, an Ace is worth 4 points, pure and simple. But a more experienced player knows that an Ace is a control, a fast trick, a card that can be used to buy time to establish other cards, a sure entry, and a card that promotes the value of other cards that accompany it. Bare Aces in a flat hand will always be less valuable than on other occasions. And an Ace in a suit of which partner is void may be worth nothing at all.

Playing with a weaker partner in a local club duplicate, you hold:

♠ A742
♡ A863
♢ A4
♣ A82

You have the point count for an opening bid of one notrump, but your high-card *structure* argues against it. Your values are *primary*, and such values often lend themselves better to suit play; it is in notrump that the *lower*-ranking intermediates assume significance, with no trump cards available to kill them off. And, more important, you have no *tenaces* whatever; if this hand is to be played at notrump, you would prefer that partner, who may have some tenace holdings, be declarer. You would open one notrump if (no pun intended) you had a couple of tens in addition to your Aces. Trying to declare notrump from your side just because partner is inexperienced is unjustified, even if you are a professional. Let him *get* some experience.

You open ONE CLUB and partner responds ONE DIAMOND. You continue with ONE HEART and partner raises to TWO HEARTS. You have enough stuff to invite game, and you choose the straightforward bid of THREE HEARTS. You might as well let partner make a decision based strictly on his point count, since any high-card values he has will probably be useful to you. And partner will pay particular attention to the quality of the trump support if the decision is close, which will suit you fine.

Partner passes over three hearts without much thought, the spade deuce is led, and you see that you are as high as you need to be when this dummy hits:

♠ 105
♡ 9742
♢ KJ73
♣ K64

☐

♠ A742
♡ A863
♢ A4
♣ A82

Plan the play.

■   ■   ■

There are several losers; three spades, two trumps at least, and maybe one in clubs. The best way to play this hand will be along the lines of a crossruff. But you cannot plan to draw no trumps at all, as you do in some crossruff situations. If you leave too many trumps at large here, the opponents will win too many tricks against you by using their trumps separately. Suppose you could arrange to draw two, and only two, rounds of trumps, leaving one high trump out. You could then start your crossruff and let the opponents take their single high trump whenever they wanted to. The way to do this is to *duck* a round of trumps and *win* the second round with your Ace.

Care must be taken that the opponents never get a chance to draw a third round of trumps with the high trump that will remain to them. So it is a good idea to *duck* the first round of spades. (The opponents will never get in with a spade trick to draw two of your trumps for one of theirs.)

Suppose they shift to a trump at trick two. You *duck*, as planned, and they will lead a second trump. If trumps go 4-1, you will have to scramble as many tricks as possible, maybe risking the diamond finesse in an effort to find a discard for your losing club. But assuming that trumps split, you will just go about your business of crossruffing and cashing winners. If the defender with three trumps has to follow to your club winners and cannot overruff you at any point during your crossruff, you will wind up with *ten* tricks.

5

As a beginner, you are told to count points for Aces, Kings, and so on, and to add points for certain distributional features. As you grow toward expert status, you begin to learn that the *quality* of your high-card values is as important as their quantity. How well the high cards and distribution complement each other, how well they mesh, or "fit," can be critical. There are a million other factors to good hand evaluation. For instance, what we call the *positional* value of your cards can change as the bidding progresses.

You are invited over to an acquaintance's to play in a home team-of-four. For my money, this is a much more pleasant way to spend an evening play bridge than trudging over to the local duplicate. The team game begins after you draw for teams and settle on a modest stake just for a little incentive. Even with a stake, it turns out to be a nice, relaxed contest. The only problem is, if you don't play well, you may not be invited back. So a good showing is imperative.

Nothing much happens for a while, and then you pick up this hand:

♠ J3
♡ KJ6
♢ AQ4
♣ 108642

Partner opens the bidding ONE SPADE. You plan to respond two clubs and try two notrump next if partner makes any minimum rebid. This sequence is about right for your invitational values. But RHO overcalls TWO HEARTS, and you have to think again. Has the value of your hand improved because of the overcall?

■   ■   ■

It has improved, most certainly. Your KJ6 of hearts, located behind the overcaller's likely AQ, is worth two tricks just as much as if you had the Ace and King! If your heart holding were Q10xx, that would be better still. You would only have to spend *two* of your high-card points to make two tricks in hearts. No doubt, you should upgrade this hand *on the bidding.* It is now worth driving to game, so you go ahead and bid THREE NOTRUMP yourself.

The heart ten is led against you, and you see:

♠ AK1084
♡ 73
◇ K96
♣ QJ7
□
♠ J3
♡ KJ6
◇ AQ4
♣ 108642

A good contract, it seems. But it's lucky that you bid game by yourself, because partner has nothing extra and wouldn't have accepted any invitations.

RHO wins the heart Ace at trick one and fires back a heart. You put in your Jack, and it holds, as LHO follows low. Plan the play from here.

■   ■   ■

The club suit could produce the tricks you need to make three notrump, but the timing is against you there. If you go after clubs, you will be down if RHO has both club honors (not unlikely on the bidding), or if they are split and LHO wins the first club and is able to produce another heart. So you decide to try spades, where four tricks will give you a total of nine. Any spade length figures to be on your left, so suppose you try the spade Jack at trick three. LHO covers with the Queen, and dummy wins, RHO playing the deuce. What do you do now?

■   ■   ■

Right. You come back to hand with a diamond and lead a second spade, intending to put in dummy's eight if LHO follows low. If the eight wins, you have nine tricks or more. If it loses, then the suit has split no worse than 4–2, and the long spade will produce the trick you need.

A *safety play* is a kind of insurance policy. You pay a premium in that you may give up the best chance to make the maximum number of tricks available from a certain combination of cards. But you guard against a devastating loss of tricks that you cannot afford. Your possible loss of tricks will be held within desirable limits. On this hand, if you play spades from the top after your Jack gets covered, you could go down (on a cold hand) if you found Q97xx on your left. The second-round finesse of the spade eight avoids this embarrassment, and assures that you'll get to play in the team game again next week.

6

Playing a match against a team that is stronger than yours, at least on paper, you hold this hand early on:

♠ A642
♡ AK3
♦ Q42
♣ A75

After a pass on your right, you start things off with ONE NOTRUMP. LHO passes, and partner deliberates, then responds TWO DIAMONDS. Lately, you and partner have been trying out a system of responses to one notrump based on *Two-Way Stayman.* You play two clubs *and* two diamonds as Stayman responses. Two clubs is used for invitational hands, while two diamonds is forcing to game and may show interest in slam. An obvious advantage of the two diamond bid is that it allows more delicate investigation in the auction. You can, for example, still play in three notrump even after you discover a fit in a major suit. A more subtle advantage is that you can respond two diamonds, Stayman, on some hands where the opponents might be able to make an effective lead directing double of a two club response.

You bid TWO SPADES, showing your suit dutifully, and partner says TWO NOTRUMP. The auction is forced to game, remember. He wants you to show another suit if you can, or rebid your spades with five of them or four very good ones. All you can do, however, is bid THREE NO-TRUMP. Partner then raises to FOUR NOTRUMP. That must be *quantitative* (that is, just a *raise* of notrump that invites slam, and not Blackwood or some other convention) and you have to decide whether to go on. What would you do?

■   ■   ■

Your point count is squarely in the middle of your notrump range, so that's no help. Your lack of intermediates and flat distribution are bad signs. But there is one big plus: most of your values are *primary*. Anytime you have a hand with lots of Aces and Kings, the hand is worth a little more than the high-card point count would indicate. The deciding factor in your decision to bid slam is that you are the underdog in this match. Maybe your best chance to sneak by is to bid a lucky slam or two. You launch into SIX NOTRUMP.

LHO leads the spade ten, and dummy is not too shabby:

♠ KJ
♡ Q105
◊ AJ105
♣ KJ62
□
♠ A642
♡ AK3
◊ Q42
♣ A75

Plan the play.

■   ■   ■

You choose to put up the spade King for starters. Your LHO is a good player, remember. It is more likely that RHO has the spade Queen singleton than that LHO would lead away from that card into your bid suit against six notrump. RHO plays low, however. Next, you lead a heart to hand and a *low* diamond to the ten. The ten holds, so you come back with another heart and lead another low diamond. This time, the King pops up on your left. If you had led the Queen of diamonds at any point, LHO would have covered to hold you to three diamond tricks. As it is, you have four diamonds, three hearts, and two spades. If you can make three, just three, club tricks, six notrump will come home. How do you tackle the club suit?

■ ■ ■

If you needed *four* tricks from clubs (as you would have if the diamond finesse had failed), you would have to find the Queen onside and the suit splitting 3-3. But for *three* club tricks, you do best to *cash* the King and Ace of clubs, and *only then* take your finesse by leading toward the Jack. You will make three club tricks whenever it is possible to do so. And this method of playing the club suit guards against losing a trick to the doubleton Queen offside and winding up with only two tricks when three were there for the taking. It's a nice *safety play* if you can see it, and it may help you to pull off an upset in this match.

7

Playing in the Blue Ribbon Pairs, you sit down against a couple of celebrities. Between them, they have a few World Championships and a few dozen National titles. There are kibitzers around the table, some of them looking on with barely-concealed admiration.

When playing against a well known player or pair, many players are beaten before they start. Intimidated by the reputation of their opponents, they roundly *over*estimate them, and imagine that they can tell what everybody at the table has after the first trick, or that they can make losers disappear into thin air, or that they can psych and otherwise operate with miraculous impunity, or that they are utterly incapable of error. None of this is true (personally, I seldom know what everybody at the table had even after the play is *over*), but the awed opponents still seem to play yellow cards, and it is no wonder the experts get more than their share of gifts. For one thing, they can overbid outrageously with little fear of being doubled.

Against a good pair, concentrate on your own game, not theirs. Play up to your capabilities. Remember first principles. For instance, always count your tricks on defense. If they bid a game against you, try to think of a way the contract will be defeated. Don't let the opponents get away with a murder you could have prevented by keeping your wits about you. The technical abilities of a name player might possibly exceed yours, but he or she has no strange powers far beyond those of mere mortals. A name player will go set in four spades if your side has four top tricks to cash and doesn't forget to take them.

The first board of the round is uneventful, and on the second one, you hold:

♠ 94
♡ Q6
♢ AKQ87542
♣ 7

With both sides vulnerable, LHO passes, partner passes, and RHO opens ONE CLUB. What should your action be?

■　　■　　■

There are many possibilities. Five diamonds could talk them out of a cold game. *One* diamond could get *you* to a cold game, which might even be three notrump. If the opening bid had been a major, you could jump to three of opening bidder's suit (!). In modern bridge, that asks partner to bid three notrump with a stopper in opener's suit! Isn't science wonderful? And, of course, you could always try a devious one notrump overcall(!) and see what action *that* stirs up.

Finally, you decide to bid FOUR DIAMONDS. This bid has a lot going for it. LHO is a passed hand and probably won't be able to act over a bid by you at the *four* level. You might even buy the contract for four diamonds if partner has a few high cards. As far as preempting all the way to the five level, you do have 11 high-card points after all, including a couple of possible defensive tricks, so it is a little presumptuous to assume that the opponents have a game and can bid it. If you get doubled at five diamonds, even a one-trick set will be bad for you if all they can make is a part score. Your pattern is poor for a leap to five diamonds anyway — you have too many losers in the major suits, and you would be bidding for an all but certain minus score. You discount as unlikely the chances that your side has a biddable game. At matchpoints, bidding game isn't the primary consideration anyhow.

All pass to four diamonds, LHO leads the club ten, and the dummy is a definite surprise:

♠ J10
♡ 8532
◊ —
♣ AKJ8642

□

♠ 94
♡ Q6
◊ AKQ87542
♣ 7

Apparently, partner refused to preempt because he had four cards in hearts. There would be more reason for him to worry about preempting *your* side if he had length in *spades*. You wouldn't want to risk missing a fit in the ranking suit; but personally, I wouldn't think twice about shooting out a three club opening with partner's hand, four small *hearts* or not.

At least you guessed not to bid five diamonds. That would certainly have been doubled. You win dummy's club Ace and continue with the King, discarding a heart. Luckily, LHO has to follow. Now you know that the trumps are splitting (RHO would have opened one diamond with four diamonds and three clubs, and would have had a five-card major suit to open in with one diamond and three clubs), but there is still danger of losing a trump trick. You will be overruffed if you try to get back to hand with a club ruff, and if you come off dummy with a major suit at this point, the opponents will cash their major suit winners and then play the club Queen, catching you in a *trump promotion.* How do you play to avoid this?

■   ■   ■

I'll bet you got this one right instinctively. Just lead a third club from dummy yourself and discard another heart when RHO produces the Queen. This *loser-on-loser* play eliminates the danger of the trump promotion by removing the dangerous club Queen from RHO's hand. Eventually, you will be able to ruff a major suit to hand, draw trumps, and make your contract on the nose.

You moved on to another table to play against some lesser lights. None of the sea of kibitzers, to your disappointment, got up to follow you. But your plus 130 was worth 8 1/2 matchpoints on a 12 top, and that was more than a little consolation.

8

One way you can invariably tell a beginner at the bridge table is the way he holds his cards. Typically, he can be seen hunched over the table, with a part of his arm touching or nearly touching it, as though nobody would bother to look at his cards, which are in plain view. Things will stay like that until somebody tells him the facts of life, or until he starts to wonder why his stiff Kings are being picked off with such monotonous regularity. Then he'll begin to clutch the cards to his chest as though they were the crown jewels.

I don't think there are many players who would go out of their way to peek, but by the same token, I don't think there are many who would pass up a free look if it were offered to them on a platter. Temptation comes to all of us in greater or lesser degrees, sometimes depending on what sort of naturally endowed equipment we have for looking. We have one personage in our club who is a regular Giraffe. Stands around six foot ten or so. Towers far above the rest of the players at the table. He just can't help but look. He leads the (bridge) League in dropping stiff Kings and has never been known to misguess a two-way finesse for a missing Queen. So when the chance comes along to give him a taste of his own medicine, you don't want to miss it.

You sit down against the Giraffe in a local Swiss Teams, and on the first board, the Giraffe, on a blind auction, plays A9x opposite Q8xx for one loser by leading low to the nine (losing to the ten), then low toward the Ace (the King came up, and he won and led low to his eight). On the next board, you sit in fourth seat with:

♠ 73
♡ A1063
◇ Q84
♣ QJ62

The Giraffe opens ONE SPADE to your left, and partner and RHO pass.
You elect to reopen with a DOUBLE. You couldn't consider a double in
the *free* position with much less than an opening bid, but a takeout double
in the *pass-out* seat can be made with as little as eight high-card points,
provided your distribution is favorable. The Giraffe passes and partner
comes to life with a TWO SPADE cue-bid. He must have passed some sort
of good hand only because no direct action was just right. You can only
bid THREE HEARTS and partner quickly raises to FOUR HEARTS. All
pass.

The Giraffe lays down the diamond Ace and partner puts down his
dummy:

♠ AQ9
♡ KQ82
◇ 752
♣ K53
□
♠ 73
♡ A1063
◇ Q84
♣ QJ62

Some players would have entered the auction directly on partner's cards
(by making a takeout double). But partner chose to wait, influenced by his
dull pattern and his defensive values, especially in the opponents' suit.

RHO plays the three of diamonds at trick one, and while the Giraffe
ponders that card, you grab his Convention Card and learn that they lead
the Ace from Ace-King-x-(x) After a while, there comes a spade shift.
You finesse dummy's Queen successfully, and draw three rounds of
trumps, finding that the Giraffe had Jxx. What would your next play be?

■   ■   ■

Of course you led a club to the King, winning, and a club back. On this trick, you played the *six* from your hand. The Giraffe's Ace came tumbling down on air, providing you with a diamond discard, and four hearts made exactly. The Giraffe shook his head as if he couldn't believe what had happened. "I saw your hand, Giraffe," you said softly. The Giraffe snorted and looked even more perplexed while the rest of the table, even including your partner, muttered dark mutterings about sharp practices. So finally you told them the facts. You saw the Giraffe's hand in your *mind*. You knew he had three trumps and at least three diamonds on the opening lead (he would have led the diamond *King* with Ace-King *alone* and RHO would have signalled for a diamond continuation if the diamond Ace had been a *singleton*), plus, almost surely, five spades for his opening bid. So the Ace of clubs just had to be guarded no more than once, and your play was a sure thing.

Nevertheless, you thought you imagined the Giraffe holding his cards a little closer to his chest on the next deal.

9

Traditionally, the first events of a weekend Sectional have been the Mens' and Womens' Pairs, held concurrently on Friday afternoon. But the Friday afternoon session is always the least well attended one, and the Mens' Pairs can turn out to be very small in a minor Sectional. In our part of the country, the two events are often combined into a "Non-Mixed Pairs." Although the top places are invariably taken by the men, grim reality being what it is, I've never heard any complaints from the distaff side. I rather think they relish the chance to disprove the theory (and that's all it is) of male superiority at the bridge table. And the event does add some variety and spice to the tournament.

Playing in a Non-Mixed, you are up against one of the few pairs of men you'll face in the session. So you need to score well. Fourth in hand, you look at:

♠ AKQ7
♡ AJ1063
♢ Q104
♣ 6

There are three quick passes and you open ONE HEART. The opponents remain silent as partner raises you to TWO HEARTS. What should you bid now?

■ ■ ■

There are two ways to look at this situation. The inexperienced player counts his high-card points, adds a few more for distribution, arrives at a figure of about eighteen or nineteen, and either jumps to four hearts or invites with three, depending on whether he is in an aggressive mood or a conservative one. But a more realistic approach, which the more seasoned player finds himself using, is to visualize some possible hands for partner. *If you can imagine some minimum hand he might hold which would make game laydown, then you can hardly do less than bid game.* Here, four hearts will be an excellent contract if partner has as little as four hearts to the King and the diamond Jack; and maybe your partner once held a better hand than that for a single raise! So you go straight to FOUR HEARTS.

The club five is led, and this dummy comes down:

♠ J63
♡ K952
◇ J83
♣ J83
□
♠ AKQ7
♡ AJ1063
◇ Q104
♣ 6

Your vision of partner's hand was sort of prophetic. He has a real dog. Some players might even respond one notrump with his cards, rather than give the more psychologically encouraging raise with so many Jacks (dubious cards for a heart contract).

RHO wins the club King at trick one and tries to cash the Ace. You ruff. Everything seems to hang on the trump position. What are your thoughts about playing that suit?

■ ■ ■

There is a really neat rule that may be applied to this situation. "Eight-ever, nine-never," the rule ordains. This rule suggests the best way to play a suit missing only the Queen. With eight cards or less, you "always" prefer to finesse in one direction or the other. But with as many as nine cards, it becomes fractionally better to play for the *drop* by cashing the Ace and King. "Eight-ever, nine-never." Even with a nine-card fit, a finesse is only a slightly inferior play mathematically, so you should be willing to finesse for a missing Queen even with nine cards in your suit if there is any indication that you should do so. Of course, the very best thing to do is to try and *figure out who has the Queen*, so that you don't have to rely on any rules. That is what you can do here.

RHO had the Ace and King of clubs and at least one of the diamond honors. LHO would have laid down a top diamond on opening lead if *he* had both of them. So the Queen of hearts is almost certainly on your left. RHO would have opened the bidding, particularly in third seat, with that card in addition to the other values you know he has. Cash the heart Ace and lead a heart to dummy, planning to finesse the nine if the Queen does not appear.

10

You and Ralph had intended to play bridge together for quite some time, but until today, you somehow never quite got around to it. You were friends, and from what little conversation you had had about bridge, your styles in the bidding seemed to be roughly compatible. You always told each other that you would just have to play "sometime" and that you would undoubtedly be a dynamite twosome. But you never played. Until today.

A strange phenomenon often occurs when a brand new partnership embarks on its maiden voyage. The partnership often does well. Sometimes very well. If I could just bottle whatever it is that makes this so, I could market it with no trouble at all. And after extensive research, I think I've discovered the cause. First, both of you are on your best behavior, anxious not to step on your new partner's toes and foul up his ego trip by being critical. Such admirable partnership rapport is not an inconsiderable factor when it comes to turning out good results. Also, you will play a fairly simple bidding system the first time out, which makes the bugaboo of a partnership mixup less likely. Knowing that you are in an unfamiliar partnership, you will lean over backwards to avoid throwing partner any curve balls in the auction. Since bridge can really be a simple game, you may reap some dividends. Throw in a little good luck, and you can be a tough act to upstage. Of course, it takes more than some momentary magic to sustain an effective partnership. Things may start to go sour as time passes and the "era of good feeling" melts away. Would that we all could retain it.

You and Ralph were really rolling along, and then you viewed this hand:

♠ AQ103
♡ J8542
♢ J1073
♣ —

Ralph opened ONE DIAMOND and RHO DOUBLED. You decided to bid ONE HEART (one spade was an alternative), intending to support diamonds later. ONE NOTRUMP was bid to your left, and Ralph came back in freely with TWO DIAMONDS. Pass on your right. What should you do?

■ ■ ■

You gave it a good deal of thought. Hands like this are more than just a matter of counting your points. You do better to try to visualize how the play will go, imagining what your losers and winners will be. Here, you figured the spade finesse would work if you needed it (and you figured to need it; Ralph rated to have at least two spades since the opponents hadn't bid that suit). Any diamond finesse would be right for you as well, since they had bid notrump in front of Ralph's suit. Best of all, you imagined partner to be *short in hearts*. RHO had some for his takeout double and LHO had some for his notrump bid, and that didn't leave many for Ralph. Also, he figured to have a few clubs, since the opposition hadn't bid that suit either. Another indication of possible heart shortage in his hand. So whatever high-card values partner had, they probably were *not* in hearts, and that *really* looked super. The longer you thought about it, the greater temptation took hold. The vision of magic fit beckoned. Finally, you gave in. Maybe your new partnership status would give you one more miraculous boost. "SIX(!) DIAMONDS." Ralph gulped and the opponents sat up like hounds on a scent. A double was almost a formality. But the combined hands were:

♠ AQ103
♡ J8542
◇ J1073
♣ —

    □

♠ 72
♡ 9
◇ AQ9642
♣ KQ73

They led a trump at him, not a bad shot. And you watched the play unfold to your satisfaction. Dummy won the first trick, as RHO refused to
cover, and Ralph carefully led a heart. RHO won and returned the King of
trumps. Ralph won it, took the spade finesse successfully, ruffed a heart,
and led to the spade Ace. He ruffed another heart, with both opponents
following, ruffed a club, ruffed a fourth heart, establishing the fifth one,
and put down the club King. LHO covered and dummy ruffed with its
last trump. Ralph then discarded his other low club on the good heart,
ruffed a spade, and claimed. Making six! A club return at trick three would
have removed one of dummy's entries prematurely, but then Ralph could
have ruffed another club in dummy. There was no way to beat the six diamond contract, even with the roach of a hand that Ralph had for his free
bid.

    When two hands are *balanced*, their high-card point count alone can
be used as a fairly reliable guide to their trick-taking potential. No more
reliable guide has been invented so far. But when two hands are *shapely*,
the *number* of high-card points they contain is anything but a good indication of how many tricks they will produce. Distribution and *particular*
high cards, especially primary values, become more important considera-
tions.

    As for you and Ralph, your debut was an unqualified success. You
wrapped up the duplicate and hurriedly made a date to play in a Regional.
Here's hoping you do as well in your next appearance.

There was a half-table at the local duplicate, so toward the end of the evening, you found that you were obliged to sit out a round. Partner exercised his options by going off to the bar for some much needed solace. And you sat down to watch somebody else cope with one of the hands you had met earlier.

♠ AQ1053
♡ A72
◇ 853
♣ K5

The subject of your scrutiny opened ONE SPADE with these cards, just as you did, and his partner, like yours, responded TWO CLUBS. Opener then rebid TWO SPADES and passed a raise to THREE SPADES with his minimum point count.

The opening lead was a diamond, and this dummy hit:

♠ KJ6
♡ 83
◇ J94
♣ AQ862
□
♠ AQ1053
♡ A72
◇ 853
♣ K5

The opponents cashed three fast diamond tricks and shifted to a heart. Declarer won and saw that the club suit could offer discards for his two heart losers. He played King of clubs, Ace of clubs, and ruffed a club high, trying to guard against a 4-2 club break. The clubs were 3-3, in fact, but when declarer next played the spade Ace and a spade toward dummy, intending to draw trumps, LHO showed out. RHO was then able to ruff one of declarer's club winners and hold him to nine tricks. Accurate bidding.

You were a lot luckier on this hand when it came to your table. The bidding was the same, except that you went on to FOUR SPADES over three. You thought your King of clubs, opposite partner's known length, was bound to be an extra valuable card. Your other side card was an Ace, which might buy you some time to set up dummy's clubs. And your trumps weren't too bad. There is more to hand evaluation than just counting high-card points, you see.

As for the play, you justified your bidding because you correctly *tested trumps* before you played clubs. If trumps had split 3-2, you planned to stop after drawing just two rounds and switch over to clubs, ruffing a third round to guard against the likely 4-2 break while a trump remained in dummy as an entry. But when trumps went 4-1, you were able to swap plans. You had to draw all the remaining trumps and hope that clubs were split 3-3. Since they were, you made your game.

12

Bridge is a partnership game, somebody once said. And there is absolutely no substitute for a partner that you can trust implicitly. A good partner can take a lot of the strain of the game off you by preventing you from making mistakes and making the correct plays easier to find. With a good partner, you can make subtle bids and plays, trusting that he will be on the ball and will work out what you are up to. Defensive signalling can be kept to a desirable minimum when your partner is capable of working out much of the hand without any assistance. All sorts of guesswork in the auction can be avoided. Slam bidding, to mention just one aspect of constructive bidding, is twice as easy.

More than anything else, a good partner gives you the confidence and the incentive to play your best bridge. You just naturally try harder with somebody with whom you have a real chance of doing well.

The best player in the club asks you to play in one of the local duplicates. Maybe he observed you working hard to master the game and liked your attitude. Needless to say, you will play as hard as you can today and try to impress him. Early in the session, the first few hands having been routine, you pick up:

♠ A83
♡ AK4
◇ 973
♣ AQ102

RHO deals and opens ONE SPADE. Your spade stopper isn't ideal; you would prefer some "soft" holding, like Q10x. But the rest of your hand is perfect for a ONE NOTRUMP overcall, so you try that. Partner lifts you to THREE NOTRUMP, the nine of spades is led, and the dummy looks like this:

♠ 752
♡ Q95
◇ AQ62
♣ J94
　□
♠ A83
♡ AK4
◇ 973
♣ AQ102

Partner's raise straight to game is worthy of attention. He has only a count of nine and is really worth only two notrump, but he knows that it pays to be aggressive in this situation. Your values are well placed *behind* the opening bidder's, and the play will be much easier for you when the location of so many of the missing high cards is obvious.

RHO plays the spade four at trick one, and you win immediately. There is no point in holding up, since LHO has no high cards and will never be on lead again. And if you were to let the spade nine hold, LHO might get the bright idea to switch to a diamond, which would be awkward for you. What do you do after winning the first trick?

■　　■　　■

First, you go to dummy with a heart and lead the *nine* of clubs for a finesse. This is the convenient way to manage the club suit so that you can take three finesses, if necessary, without getting tangled up. (If you lead the Jack and unblock the ten, RHO could cover the nine later (with K87x) and promote himself a trick. If you do not unblock, you will have to win a second finesse in your hand.) The club nine holds, and you continue with the Jack, and then a low one to the Queen. RHO's King finally falls under the club Ace, while LHO has pitched a heart and the spade six. Next, you cash your other two hearts, and RHO throws a spade on the last one. Now what should you do?

■   ■   ■

An easier *endplay* could hardly be imagined. RHO is marked with the diamond King for his opening bid, so you just get out with one of your spades. RHO can cash just two more spades, and then he must lead into dummy's diamond tenace. So you wind up making four, for what should be a fine score. If RHO had discarded a diamond on the third heart, you would lead to the diamond Ace. You know that RHO had four clubs, two hearts, and five spades (surely he would have opened one club with four cards in each black suit), therefore two diamonds, and the diamond King would now fall for you.

"Nicely done," your partner says, giving you a nod of approval. You are definitely on your way up. It occurs to you that another nice thing about a good partner is that he can appreciate your excellent declarer play.

13

You're trying to qualify for the Knockouts, and it may be a close proposition, especially if you mismanage this vulnerable game hand. As dealer, you pick up:

♠ KJ5
♡ 742
◊ AJ105
♣ A43

You open ONE DIAMOND and partner responds TWO CLUBS. Faced with an uncomfortable rebid problem, you decide to try TWO NOTRUMP instead of raising clubs. Your distribution, at least, is as notrumpish as it can get, and you will get your hands on the dummy in any notrump game. THREE DIAMONDS from partner. Now you can bid THREE SPADES to show where your major-suit strength is concentrated and stay below three notrump at the same time. Partner nods appreciatively and signs off in THREE NOTRUMP; you have nothing more to say.

LHO leads the seven of spades, and dummy comes down with:

♠ 864
♥ AQ
♦ K742
♣ KQ72

□

♠ KJ5
♥ 742
♦ AJ105
♣ A43

Not so bad. RHO plays the spade ten at trick one, and you win your Jack. Plan your play from here.

■　　■　　■

It looks as though LHO led from a spade suit headed by the Ace and Queen, and is now lurking behind you with his tenace. It would probably be fatal if RHO ever got in to play a spade through you, so you plan to make an "avoidance" play by taking your diamond finesse through RHO. (This is the best way to attack the diamond suit anyway; you can handle Q9xx on your right, but not on your left.) When you play a diamond to the King and a diamond back to your Jack, LHO wins the Queen.

And now comes a disconcerting turn of events. Your LHO shifts to a *heart*. At this point, you have eight tricks ready to cash. The ninth one could come from a 3-3 split in the club suit, or a successful heart finesse. Your opponent's heart shift has effectively *deprived you of the opportunity to try both chances*. You must decide right this minute whether to stake your contract on the heart finesse (unpleasant, since you will be *swiftly* down if it doesn't work), or try to find the clubs splitting (not as good a percentage shot as the heart finesse). I can almost guarantee you that whichever play you choose will be wrong, whereas the other one would have worked.

Maybe you won't qualify for the Knockouts, but you might learn something from this hand. You should cash three rounds of clubs *before* you make your diamond play. You will find out how many club tricks are available to you on this hand, enabling you to tell whether the heart finesse will be a necessary evil if you lose a diamond finesse and take only three diamond tricks.

14

Along with old Blackwood, the Stayman convention is almost universally played. This convention, which has its origins somewhere in the mists of contract bridge antiquity, was developed by George Rapee and others in the 1940s, and bears the name of former World Champion Sam Stayman, one of the more interesting personalities we have in the world of tournament bridge.

As I tell my Beginning Bridge classes, Stayman is theoretically sound and well worth knowing about, even for those who are just starting to learn the language of bidding. (There are always those who rebel instinctively against the notion that a bid might possibly have some meaning assigned to it other than its natural one; some of these people, at least, can be taught the logic of a bid like Stayman. But others start out by asking if the Stayman convention is anything like the VFW Convention, and that's when I know I'm in a lot of trouble with this group.)

Stayman is most commonly used to uncover a 4-4 fit in a major suit after an opening bid in notrump. Possession of a trump suit frequently makes the play safer and easier to control, and may allow declarer to make crucial extra tricks by using his trumps. A 4-4 fit is excellent for producing these extra tricks, since declarer can ruff something in *either* hand and still retain four trumps in the other hand to draw trumps with.

There are also other situations in which Stayman is a useful gadget to have around. Playing in the quarterfinals of a rough, tough Knockout event, you hold this hand:

♠ KQJ53
♥ 6
♦ Q73
♣ 9742

Partner opens ONE NOTRUMP, showing 15-17 HCP. Without Stayman, you would have an impossible problem. Game could be cold, so you are too strong to sign off with two spades, but a *three* spade response would be forcing to game, and you aren't strong enough to force. Use of Stayman, however, *implies at least interest in game,* so you can compromise and start with TWO CLUBS. TWO DIAMONDS from partner. Now you bid TWO SPADES. Partner knows that you have at least five spades (if you had only four, you wouldn't bother to bid spades, since you know now there could be no fit), and invitational strength (since you used Stayman instead of bidding two spades directly).

Partner now bids THREE DIAMONDS, and you have to consider again. What could three diamonds mean? Could partner want to play the hand at diamonds? No, he wouldn't suddenly decide to explore for new trump suits at this stage. Matter of fact, he would just go back to notrump with hands lacking support for your suit. He must have *spades*! The three diamond bid is an attempt to get to a spade game, by showing you where some of his values are concentrated. Knowing that, how do you feel about your game chances?

■   ■   ■

Well, your diamond Queen suddenly looks like a golden card and some of your losers (in diamonds) are no longer a worry. Perhaps partner has a doubleton club, or no wasted values in hearts! You leap to FOUR SPADES.

LHO leads the Queen of hearts, and you are faced with this:

♠ A107
♡ A83
◇ AKJ
♣ 10653
□
♠ KQJ53
♡ 6
◇ Q73
♣ 9742

Alas, the wrong contract. Three notrump is cold, four spades is uncertain. There is fearful *duplication of values* in the minor suits. (This condition, which is sometimes hard to diagnose, occurs when some of your high cards and distribution fail to complement each other. A King-Queen opposite a singleton might be wasted cards in a suit contract. And here, partner's Jack of diamonds might as well be the deuce.) Perhaps partner should have gambled out three notrump with his very flat distribution.

As for your making four spades, you will need to scrape together a trick in clubs, and a 3-2 split will be necessary. Furthermore, *trumps* will have to split 3-2 for you, or else you will be out of control by the time you finally get a club trick established. Keeping in mind that the opponents will force you to ruff hearts every time they gain the lead, how will you conduct the play?

■   ■   ■

Even assuming all the favorable breaks, there are still precautions to be taken. If you draw three rounds of trumps and then start clubs, you will surely be forced out of control.

The opponents will lead hearts each of the three times they win a club trick, and you will have only two trumps left in hand to cope with them. You must set up your club trick *first*, then. The opponents will be able to force you in your hand twice, but by the time they win their third club trick, the *dummy* will be out of hearts and will be able to ruff any further heart leads. You will be able to save three trumps in your hand and hope to keep control.

There is an important principle here that extends to the play of many hands. If you are in a tough contract, and you anticipate lots of problems in the play, especially keeping control of the trump suit, *your first idea should be to set up your side suit*. Don't worry about playing another suit with some trumps still out against you. If there are control problems, the danger of opposing ruffs is a secondary consideration.

15

The Mixed Pairs has always been viewed as a microcosmic Battle of the Sexes. The male half of the partnership is alleged to assert his virility by bidding lots of notrump and a good deal of everything else, while the female half sits benignly by, ready only to shake a doleful head when some of her better half's operations go astray. I doubt that everyone would agree that this scenario is the correct one, especially in these days of sexual equality. And it's still a partnership game, even if you're playing with your husband or wife. But the Mixed-up Pairs, as it is somewhat derisively referred to, does produce more than its share of strange results and strange happenings. That's not to say it isn't a great event to play in. Around here, many of the ladies wear those beautiful long dresses for the evening session, and there is usually a dance or a *soirée* of some kind after the game is over.

Playing in a Mixed, your side is not vulnerable, and you hear your distaff partner open ONE HEART. RHO passes and you gaze at this collection:

♠ AJ10
♡ 952
♢ 1063
♣ 9742

The textbooks say a response should be given with six or more points here. But there are certain five-point hands that are worth a bid. In this case, you have an Ace (a sure trick), and a Jack that is worth more since the Ace supports it. Game could easily be cold, and a pass will let the opponents come in too cheaply anyhow, so you decide to bid. Should you raise hearts with your three-card support or bid one notrump?

■   ■   ■

ONE NOTRUMP is probably better. This is not a good hand for hearts, with no shape; and two hearts, even though it suggests the same amount of strength as a one notrump response, is psychologically more likely to encourage partner to act aggressively. Personally, I'd consider one notrump here even with one *more* heart and one less club, in order to slow things down while retaining a chance to get to game if partner has a really good hand. (An eccentric one notrump response with concealed hearts has a possible added advantage; it may cause the opponents to misjudge your heart fit, and therefore, their own offensive prospects.)

Over your one notrump, partner jumps to THREE CLUBS. You are still interested in staying low, so you take a preference to THREE HEARTS instead of supporting the clubs. At this, partner goes into her own private world and eventually surfaces with . . . THREE NOTRUMP. You can't see any reason not to sit for the cheapest game, so the auction grinds to a halt.

The King of diamonds is the ominous opening lead, and the dummy is a little strange. Just about right for the Mixed Pairs.

♠ K
♡ AKQ873
◇ 972
♣ AQ5

□

♠ AJ10
♡ 952
◇ 1063
♣ 9742

Partner later explained that she thought she was too good for a three heart rebid and not good enough in tricks for four hearts. Then, having overbid her high cards with the devious jump to three clubs, she was afraid to try the *ten*-trick heart game. The machinations of the female bridge mind.

Whether by luck or feminine intuition, you seem to have arrived in the best contract. The opponents can cash only four diamond tricks, ending on your right, and then they switch to a spade. How should you plan the play to make your partner happy?

■   ■   ■

There are two options, and the question must be decided strictly on an actuarial basis, as there is nothing else to go on. You can (1) win the spade King and cash two top hearts. If hearts are 2–2, you enter your hand with the third heart to take the spade Ace, and the club Ace and the rest of the hearts will produce nine tricks. Or, (2) you can *overtake* the spade King with the Ace and finesse in clubs. This will result in down two if your finesse fails, for the opponents will cash the spade Queen as well, but your matchpoint result probably won't be affected much. Down one *or* two won't be very good for you, since most pairs won't reach game with your cards. Your main consideration should be finding the best play for nine tricks.

This is an easy problem in *percentage play*. The club finesse will work one half the time, while the chances of getting to your hand with the third heart depend on a 2-2 split there, a 40 percent shot. You can see, then, that overtaking the spade King is the superior line.

16

The bidding works like this: you and I exchange information through the bids we make. Each bid has a meaning, often a narrowly defined meaning. At some point during our exchange, one of us will make a bid that *limits his strength*. The other player then becomes the "captain" of the partnership, and must decide at what level the contract should play. If you open one spade, for instance, and I raise to two spades, showing six to nine points and some spade support, you are captain. You now know what our combined assets add up to, and you can tell if game or slam is a possibility.

Limiting your hand early in the auction has some obvious advantages (especially if the hand is very weak and you will only be able to take *one* descriptive bid). Suppose you could make just one bid and not only limit your high-card strength but describe your approximate pattern as well. You could relax for the rest of the auction and let partner sweat out what to do. That's what partners are for anyway. You'd have to come out ahead if the bidding were always that simple. And that's why you should invariably open one notrump whenever you have the right strength and pattern.

Some players have a pathological fear of opening one notrump with a five-card major suit. The only logical reason for this is that they fear a superior major-suit contract might be missed. Maybe so, but it's just as easy to argue that some good notrump spots will go by the boards if you avoid such prosaic sequences as one notrump-three notrump.

Besides, what do you do about opening a hand like:

♠ A8
♡ AK753
♢ Q63
♣ K92

■   ■   ■

You say you'd open one heart? OK, what is partner's most likely response? One spade, right? Now what? One notrump? Shows a balanced *minimum* opening. Two notrump? Shows about 19 balanced. Two hearts? Shows a minimum and suggests six or more hearts. Two clubs?? Two diamonds?? Echhh!

With five *spades* in a balanced sixteen or so points, you might get away with a one spade opening. You can bid two notrump over a two level response (if that promises extra values), or jump to three notrump, hoping you can fight partner off if he gets excited and tries for slam. But with 2-5-3-3 shape, you almost *have* to open one notrump to avoid the looming rebid problems.

On this occasion, partner raises your ONE NOTRUMP opening to THREE NOTRUMP. You have had a simple, unrevealing auction. The ten of diamonds is led, and partner tables this, with a little guilty squirming thrown in for effect. You have arrived in three notrump with a *nine*-card heart fit. Scandalous!

♠ J107
♥ 10842
♦ A5
♣ QJ103
□
♠ A8
♥ AK753
♦ Q63
♣ K92

You duck the opening lead, RHO plays the Jack, and you win the Queen. Partner traded heavily on the presumed value of the tens to raise you to game. How do you plan the play to make partner look good?

■   ■   ■

If hearts are 2-2, you can make five with no trouble. But if the suit does not split, you will have to knock out the club Ace as well as set up the hearts before nine tricks are available. If the opponents are going to get in *twice*, they may get their diamond suit set up and cashed. So your correct timing of the play may make all the difference.

Diamonds may well be 6-2 from RHO's play to the first trick. Say you lead a club to begin with. RHO might win the Ace and return his last diamond. Then, if LHO had three hearts for an entry, you would go down. It looks like what you need to do is knock out whatever entry LHO has to his diamonds *early*, before they get established. (You would like to see LHO in the lead early for another reason also: a *spade switch* by *RHO* might be as devastating as a diamond return; but you can probably cope with a spade switch from your *left*.) But, which entry does LHO have?

To find out, play off the top hearts. Unblock the eight- or ten-spot from dummy. If LHO has a heart stopper, continue the suit to dislodge what you hope is his only entry. If RHO is the one with three hearts, though, you switch over to clubs. If LHO has the club Ace, you need to get it out of his hand early in the play. The full deal was:

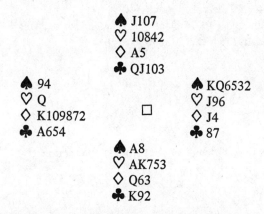

```
                    ♠ J107
                    ♡ 10842
                    ◇ A5
                    ♣ QJ103
   ♠ 94                            ♠ KQ6532
   ♡ Q                             ♡ J96
   ◇ K109872        □              ◇ J4
   ♣ A654                          ♣ 87
                    ♠ A8
                    ♡ AK753
                    ◇ Q63
                    ♣ K92
```

You made three notrump, much to the disgust of the pairs who were in four hearts. The nine of spades was led against that contract; Jack, Queen, *Ace*. Declarer cashed the two high trumps and led a club, but LHO won, led a spade to partner, and the diamond return established four tricks for the defense. The only declarer to *make* four hearts led the *ten of hearts* from dummy at one point. When RHO covered (it was hard not to), the Queen and Jack of trumps crashed on the same trick, and declarer was able to pick up the trump suit without loss by finessing against the nine later.

17

Lately, the ACBL has taken to running "Flighted" events at many of its tournaments. Anybody with more than a certain number of Master Points is required to play in "Flight A," while the rest of the field is forced, or maybe allowed, to play in "Flight B" or "C." This scheme adds variety to the tournament, provides tougher competition for those who want it, and does a little something to recognize the huge gulf that distinguishes the Life Masters of widely different skills.

Playing in a Flight A Open Pairs (your partner has 751 Master Points, and the cut-off was 750), you pick up:

♠ 10753
♡ AQ954
◇ Q5
♣ KJ

There are three passes around to you. What is your action?

■ ■ ■

This is a reasonable opening in any position, with the length in the majors. And it is especially important to open at duplicate bridge; there may be a major-suit partial available to your side, and if you pass the hand out, you risk getting a very round zero. If you had the minor suits instead, you might toss the hand in, but not so here. ONE HEART, you open. LHO passes and partner leaps to THREE DIAMONDS! Has a hidden Ace been discovered? Should you bid again?

■ ■ ■

In a way, partner really has "discovered" some extra strength. A jump shift by a passed hand can only mean that partner now thinks more of his hand than he did before he heard your one heart opening. He must have a good *heart* fit, and his hand has improved, so that it is now worth as much as an opening bid.

Your Queen of diamonds looks good, and there is a fair chance that partner is short in spades, so you decide that there are prospects for a top in FOUR HEARTS. All pass, LHO bangs down the spade Ace, and the table displays:

♠ K8
♡ J1062
◇ AK842
♣ 74
□
♠ 10753
♡ AQ954
◇ Q5
♣ KJ

You seem to be in a good game. RHO plays the nine of spades at trick one, and drops the Queen on a spade continuation. Playing for the maximum, you pass the heart Jack at trick three. But LHO wins the King and leads a low spade. When you ruff with the ten of hearts, RHO discards a low club. You draw two more trumps (unfortunately, LHO had the King alone), exhausting dummy in the process, and play diamonds. More bad luck. LHO follows with the Jack on the second diamond and discards a low club on the third one. You discard your losing spade and must now guess clubs to make this contract. RHO plays a low club when you lead that suit from dummy. So which club do you play?

■   ■   ■

Fortunately, this isn't any tough guess, at least not if you've been paying attention and counting. LHO failed to open the bidding and has shown up with the spade Ace and Jack, the heart King, and the diamond Jack. With the club Ace in addition to all that, he would have had thirteen high-card points, and presumably would have opened the bidding (especially since he had a spade suit). So you go up with your *King* of clubs, and claim four when it holds.

As it happened, you would have been better off to start trumps by leading low to your Queen. With both the Jack and ten remaining in dummy, you would have had an extra entry to set up diamonds against a 4-2 split, and the club "guess" would have proved unnecessary.

As to the way the play actually went, reflect on this. Card-placing is supposed to be strictly the domain of the expert, who is thought in some quarters to carry a crystal ball around, stuffed in a left back pocket. But the elements of card-placing are really only simple techniques of *counting* and *inference* that can be easily applied by anyone who is willing to take the time to think of them. And that includes *you*.

18

This hand, which might be entitled "The Case of the Missing Suit," comes from an important match in one of the National Team Championships many years ago. See if you can do as well as the expert player who actually bid the hand and then declared it.

♠ AKQ4
♡ Q109652
◇ A63
♣ —

Neither side is vulnerable. Your partner opens ONE DIAMOND and raises your ONE HEART response to TWO HEARTS. What would you bid now?

■　　■　　■

Blackwood is no help at all here. If partner showed one Ace, you would have not the faintest idea of how many hearts to bid. You could beat around several bushes here, but the key to the whole problem is partner's *trump* holding. Luckily, there is a gadget available that will let you find out what partner has in trumps. This gadget, called the Grand Slam Force, is a very old convention. It was originated in the early days of contract bridge, around 1930. The GSF works like this: A *jump* to five notrump asks partner to bid a grand slam if he holds *two of the top three honors in the agreed trump suit*. There are many variations. For example, if you have used Blackwood, you cannot follow up with five notrump, intending it as the Grand Slam Force. Partner would think you were asking for Kings. If you wanted to use the GSF, you would have to bid six of a new suit, and show your interest in seven that way. In some other cases, you can bid *five* of a new suit, inducing partner to convert to five no-trump; then you go ahead and bid six of your agreed suit, and partner knows you are interested in seven, since you took a roundabout route to get to six.

So you bid FIVE NOTRUMP here, and partner brightens and bids SEVEN HEARTS, to which all pass. The opening lead is a trump, and you see that the contract is not quite as laydown as you had hoped:

♠ 952
♡ AK73
◇ KJ10752
♣ —

□

♠ AKQ4
♡ Q109652
◇ A63
♣ —

Both void in clubs?? You would think the opponents would have been heard from, with their thirteen-card fit. Maybe they're asleep. You win the trump lead in hand and draw a second round, noting that LHO shows out. Why couldn't they have led a club? You could have ruffed in dummy, discarded a diamond from your hand, and claimed. But now you have to find the diamond Queen for yourself.

Putting off the evil moment as long as possible, you play four rounds of spades, ruffing the fourth in dummy. LHO follows twice and RHO follows to all four rounds. A few more rounds of trumps accomplish nothing, as the opponents stoically discard clubs. How do you finally resolve the guess for your grand slam?

■　　■　　■

You know that LHO had one trump and two spades. And now really, where *are* all those clubs? How do you think the thirteen missing clubs are divided? Suppose somebody had an *eight*-card suit. *Surely* they would have bid with eight clubs. The opponents' silence is hard enough to understand as it is. The clubs must be split 7-6. And if LHO had only six clubs, he would have four diamonds; RHO, with his diamond void, would have probably doubled the slam for the lead of dummy's first bid suit.

So, confidently, you play the diamond Ace and a diamond. LHO follows low, and you close your eyes and call for the Jack. When you open them, there is a club played to your right, and all is well. You win 11 IMPS, since only a small slam was bid at the other table.

Note that, as declarer, you should try to put off any crucial guesses as long as possible, so that some information may have a chance to come your way during the play. In deciding on your line of play, a *count*, even an *inferential* count, of the opponents' distribution can make your task a lot easier. And in a grand slam, you want to grasp every straw.

19

In modern tournament bridge, most of the contestants play *weak* two bids. The old strong two bid has been ushered out, at least in the top three suits. Two *clubs* is still a strong opening, but *all* of your strong hands are opened with two clubs. Your later bidding clarifies what kind of strong opening you have. Openings of two spades, hearts, or diamonds show a-round nine or ten high-card points and a good six-card suit. The weak two bid is a mild preempt and a descriptive action as well. If you play weak twos, you get more for your tournament entry fee, because they enable you to get into the auction on some hands that you would have to pass otherwise.

No matter what your preference in two bids, a strong, forcing opening still requires nine or ten or more playing tricks, and excellent defensive values. Too many players are inclined to force to game with only a large assortment of high cards, without knowing where the *tricks* to make game are coming from. *Whether you choose to open with a forcing bid is more a matter of playing tricks and defensive strength than high-card points.*

Indulging in a quiet evening of rubber bridge at home, you hold:

♠ AKJ753
♡ AQ63
♢ AK
♣ 4

Are you worth a forcing opening?

■   ■   ■

You can count nine playing tricks, all right. Five or six in spades (let's call it 5 1/2), one or two in hearts (1 1/2), two in diamonds. Your defensive values are formidable as well, so you open TWO CLUBS. Partner responds TWO DIAMONDS, the negative reply to your forcing opening, and you bid a clarifying TWO SPADES. Partner says TWO NO-TRUMP, suggesting a balanced pile of nothing. Next, you try THREE HEARTS. Perhaps partner has four cards in that suit. Over this, partner huddles and comes out with FOUR SPADES. Should you make another move?

■   ■   ■

Remember, partner began with two bids that showed abject weakness, and he expects you to keep that in mind. Over three hearts, he might feel obliged to bid *four* spades with any hand containing a few spades and some sign of a trick. Since even four spades may not be laydown, you PASS.

The club Ace is opened, and upon seeing dummy, you are glad that you didn't get carried away.

♠ Q62
♡ 742
◇ 8652
♣ Q63
  □
♠ AKJ753
♡ AQ63
◇ AK
♣ 4

You see what I mean about the auction? Partner was scared to bid only three spades at his last turn. He thought there was a chance you might pass, fearing that he had a completely hopeless hand, maybe with a doubleton spade. Many pairs do play that a two club opening is absolutely forcing only to three of a major. (Incidentally, do you know how *your* favorite partner plays it?)

After winning the first trick, LHO continues with a low club. You play the Queen from dummy and ruff RHO's King. A spade to the Queen is followed by the heart finesse and your Queen wins the trick. You cash another high trump, and RHO shows out. You are safe for the contract, at least, but before finishing the play, you check the scorepad and note that you can eke out an extra point by making an overtrick in this contract. So it is your duty to partner to try and make five if possible. How do you play from here?

■　■　■

If hearts are 3-3, there will be no problem. If LHO had just two hearts, there will also be no problem, since you will *never* make five—LHO will overruff dummy if you try to ruff your fourth heart there. So you might as well assume that LHO has four hearts and RHO has Kx. If you take your heart Ace and lead a third round, LHO will be able to win and return his last trump, leaving you stranded with a heart loser. To make five, you lead a *low* heart on the second round, playing RHO for the bare King.

This is a simple example of *playing on an assumption*. You play the hand assuming that RHO has Kx of hearts, because that is the only case where it can matter what you do.

20

It's not generally known, but in some dark and dreary places, the only bridge is the one over the local river. The story of how you got marooned in one of these forgotten burgs is too depressing to go into in any detail. But there you were, laid up in a dingy motel, waiting for the morrow when you could get back to the real world. There was no duplicate game in town (or much of anything else, for that matter; when you asked the motel desk clerk what there was to do, he said you had two choices: you could either watch the traffic light change or listen to the cars rust) So you had to improvise. You took out a deck of cards and began to deal out hands, just to see if something interesting might turn up. This was the first deal in the match between you and yourself.

The dealer's hand was:

♠ KQ
♡ A1063
◇ AK92
♣ A94

You figured it was a ONE DIAMOND opening. Two notrump didn't appeal to you because of the doubleton King-Queen, and the lack of playing tricks otherwise. The opposite hand:

♠ A9853
♡ 952
◇ 63
♣ QJ6

So you responded ONE SPADE. Should opener rebid two hearts or two notrump now? TWO NOTRUMP had to be better, you thought. Two hearts would imply longer diamonds than hearts. And two hearts would really be unnecessary; responder couldn't have four hearts unless he had five or more spades (he would respond "up-the-line" with one heart if he held four cards in each major). But if responder did have, say, five spades and four hearts, he would bid three *hearts* over opener's two notrump rebid.

You noted that responder would raise two notrump to THREE NOTRUMP, so game would be reached with no problem. And a surreptitious peak at opening leader's hand revealed that the club deuce would be his choice. So now you stopped to consider how the play in three notrump would go. (Plan the play yourself, dear reader.)

♠ A9853
♡ 952
◇ 63
♣ QJ6
□
♠ KQ
♡ A1063
◇ AK92
♣ A94

Clearly, the spades must provide the bulk of the tricks to make this game. And there must be a sure entry to the spade suit. So declarer must play *low* from dummy at trick one, and, regardless of what RHO plays, win the *Ace*. With both club honors still in dummy and two small ones saved in the closed hand, the sure entry is there. Now, how to go after the spades?

■   ■   ■

If the contract were *four* notrump, you'd have to go all out, cashing the top spades in hand, getting to dummy in clubs, and hoping to take five spade tricks with the aid of a 3-3 break. But in *three* notrump, you don't need the whole spade suit to come in; you only need *four tricks*. Your best chance? Cash the spade King and *overtake* the Queen. If spades are 3-3, this play will only cost you an overtrick. You will still make three by conceding a spade and setting up the suit. The times you gain is when somebody has the doubleton Jack or ten of spades. In that case, their honor will fall on the second spade, and now you can lead the nine from dummy and force out the other honor. This way, you will make four spade tricks, and your contract, even against some common 4-2 breaks. If they win the third spade on your right and shift to hearts instead of returning clubs, you must duck, of course, to avoid the prospect of losing three hearts, a club, and a spade.

You dealt out a few more hands, but none was as interesting as that first one. And pretty soon, you decided that you were getting a little sleepy, and the game was too tough to play in anyway, with you in charge of all four hands. You pulled the covers over your head. And the next bridge you saw was the following morning, crossing the local river on the way out of town.

21

You came by the club only to kibitz a few hands because you had another engagement that afternoon. But one of the players was delayed. A small fire had destroyed two rooms of his house and his pet aardvark was laid up at the vet's with a touch of smoke inhalation, so he would be an hour or so late for the game. You tried your best to become invisible, but you were impressed into service as an emergency replacement anyway. Just temporary, of course. It really would be impolite to refuse when there is no other kibitzer in the club.

At tournaments, the call often goes out for someone to fill in for a player who is indisposed. Personally, I would just as soon not be responsible for part of somebody else's score. There is a tendency to approach the task lightly and not give your 100 percent best effort when you are playing for persons unknown and not yourself. The prospect of a hideous misunderstanding with a strange partner is always to be feared.

The last time I filled in for somebody, I played a dummy absolutely great (in an uncharacteristic performance), and earned a sure top. And then I went back to watching. But soon, there came *another* call for a fill-in pair. I threw up my hands, deciding that fate intended me to play bridge that day and volunteered for the whole rest of the session. Then they told me that the pair I would be subbing for was the pair I had played the first round *against*. So the first thought that came to mind was, was I stuck with the zero that I had given myself on the first round?

Back at the club, you find yourself facing a fierce-looking little old lady named Bertha, who looks as though she has some well-cherished ideas about bidding. The first board bears this out. You pick up:

♠ AJ8632
♡ A5
◇ K63
♣ 93

Neither side is vulnerable, and LHO opens THREE HEARTS. The little old lady looks at her cards and snaps out a DOUBLE. You see no reason to be scientific about it and roar into Blackwood. When partner admits to two Aces, you close the auction with SIX SPADES.

A heart is led and Bertha displays this dummy with obvious pride. "Got a good hand for you, partner." You return a sickly smile.

♠ K104
♡ 1063
◇ AJ72
♣ AQ5
□
♠ AJ8632
♡ A5
◇ K63
♣ 93

With partner looking at you expectantly, like she wants you to hurry up and claim, you'd better find a way to make this somehow. RHO plays the Queen at trick one. How do you plan to play?

■   ■   ■

As far as the trump position goes, this is no time for "eight-ever, nine-never." With LHO thought to have seven hearts and RHO just one, the odds shift in favor of a finesse through RHO. (The odds on playing for the drop with nine cards missing the Queen are only fractionally better than taking a finesse, even in the absence of any information about the distribution.) Also, the three heart bidder will usually have a singleton somewhere, and he might have chosen to *lead* any minor-suit singleton against your slam, rather than a heart away from his King-Jack. I would make the finesse through RHO about a four-to-one favorite. And so it proves. You win the first trick, play a spade to the King and a spade back to your Jack, and LHO discards a heart. That's one hurdle cleared. You draw the last trump. Now you can make this with a little good luck and a good guess. If RHO has Qxx of diamonds, then three rounds of that suit will endplay him. Of course, *LHO* could have Qxx of diamonds, and then you could make your twelve tricks by simply taking a finesse.

Before you think about it too long, go ahead and lead the diamond King and another diamond toward dummy. LHO nicely follows with the Queen on the second diamond. Now how should you continue?

■   ■   ■

Neither one of the first two plans you had in mind will work, but there is a simple alternative. You continue with the diamond Jack and LHO pitches another heart. On the lead of dummy's fourth diamond, RHO plays the ten and you . . . pitch your losing heart. RHO is left on play with only clubs left in his hand and has to lead into the ol' pickle barrel, giving you your slam-going trick.

Luckily, the aardvark recovered and the tardy player came in a couple of hands later, so your declarer play didn't get the workout you anticipated it might. That might have been just as well. "Thank you for being my partner," says Bertha. You nod, all the while hoping that her new partner, whoever he is, can play the socks off the dummy.

22

I read somewhere that, at any given time, almost a million people are taking bridge instruction at some level. For my money, the hardest class to teach is the one for the absolute beginners. An experienced player has all these concepts that are strictly second nature to him, and now he has to find the words to describe them to a group of people, some of whom may never have held a deck of cards before. Could you, without difficulty, make someone understand what a *trick* is? I spend more time preparing for a Beginning course than any other.

In a Beginning class, the students have to have general rules pounded into them because they lack the experience to solve problems without some handy rules to guide them. Saddle them with too many fine points and exceptions, and they rapidly become confused and may lose interest.

But then comes the next stage, the feared *Intermediate* class. I think a lot of bridge teachers, earnest and patient people though they are, fall down on the job a little here. They teach the Intermediate class the same way they teach the beginners. Rules. Lots of 'em. Maybe they're just not equipped to do it any other way. The problem, of course, is that nobody can (really) play bridge by strict adherence to any set of rules. This is a *thinking* game. You can't expect to enjoy yourself and get the most from the time you spend at the bridge table unless you learn how to think like a bridge player. So my perception of an Intermediate class is that this is where thought processes should begin to develop. Part of every class should be devoted to logical reasoning at the table. Could be you think that a typical Intermediate group can't handle stuff like drawing inferences from the bidding. Maybe so, but if there is no spark of interest, then my bet is that nothing much would result from inflicting them with a lot of memory work instead. There would be no prospective bridge players in that group no matter what you tried. Why not be an optimist and expect a lot from your class? Let's face it. If you stand up and spout off a long stream of facts, the class isn't going to remember much of what you had to say. They are there, basically, to have a good time, not to listen to an academic-sounding dissertation. I think that, if you are a realist, all you can hope to do in most bridge classes is *inspire.* You show the class something about what a beautiful game this is and how mentally stimulating it can be, and you hope they decide they want to become bridge players.

You decided to invest in a few lessons from a prominent teacher and successful player, fully prepared to back out if he started talking about cover-an-honor-with-an-honor. But it turns out that his idea is to have you observe the thought processes of a good player in the hope that some of it might rub off on you. (He assumes that you had a solid grasp of the fundamentals.) On the first night, he gives you this problem:

"You're playing in a matchpoint game," he says, "and you get dealt this hand:"

♠ A5
♡ QJ10753
◇ 852
♣ Q6

"Both sides are red. RHO deals and passes and you decide not to open a weak two hearts because you have too many points outside the heart suit and no distribution, and because one opponent has already passed. LHO opens ONE DIAMOND, partner passes, and RHO responds TWO CLUBS. Now you decide to come in with TWO HEARTS. This is a dangerous bid, because you could get doubled and get your head handed to you. But you shut out a two diamond rebid on your left and you may get partner off to the best lead if they wind up in notrump, so it does have a little something going for it. LHO raises to THREE CLUBS, and partner raises you to THREE HEARTS. All pass."

"They lead the diamond Ace, and this is what you see":

♠ 1072
♡ A982
◇ Q107
♣ K104
□
♠ A5
♡ QJ10753
◇ 852
♣ Q6

"They continue with the diamond King at trick two, with RHO playing high-low, and RHO ruffs the third round with the six of hearts. Back comes a spade and you win. If you can get out of this for down one, you should be OK matchpoint-wise, since they can surely make something.

When you lead the Queen of hearts, LHO plays the four. Should you finesse or go up? And please don't tell me that LHO would have covered with the King if he'd had it."

■　　■　　■

You tried to work it out. You knew that LHO had started with five diamonds, and at least three clubs for his raise. The spades . . . And the answer hit you like a lamp switched on. The spades were, had to be, 4-4. LHO would have opened one spade with five spades and five diamonds. RHO would have responded one spade with a five-card suit! So LHO could not have another heart.

"I play the Ace," you said. And your brilliant rationale came tumbling out. "I think maybe there is hope," said your mentor with just a trace of a smile. And you decided you were going to like the lessons.

23

Down from the bridge club, there hangs a blinking neon sign that proclaims FOOD-BEVERAGES. After the game, the bridge players usually migrate in that direction en masse, where they proceed to seat themselves up and down the long tables and argue and swap stories and commiserate and laugh and drink large pitchers of beer long into the night.

Behind the bar, forever cleaning his pitchers and glasses, presides a fixture known to all and sundry as, simply, Marvin. Marvin is a special bartender, much beloved by the bridge players because he has become an expert. Not an expert at bridge, but an expert at tactfully listening to the tragedies of any of the club members who need somebody to serve as a wailing wall. When Marvin first began to work at the little bar, he didn't even know there was such a game as bridge. But after being around a bunch of raucous bridge players for a while, he caught on and then some. Now we treat him almost as an equal.

You walked into the bar ahead of the crowd. You hadn't had that good a game, so you didn't bother to wait for the scores. You would hear about them soon enough. For the time being, you pulled up a stool to the bar, where Marvin was frying hamburgers in anticipation of the bridge players' impending arrival.

"How'd it go?" Marvin asked you. "Poorly," you moaned. "You know what, Marvin? You can always have 180 in a matchpoint game no matter how many bad breaks you get, but you're not going to have any *big* game without a little help." "I know what you mean," said Marvin, even though he had never played in a real bridge game, so far as we knew. "Look at this," you continued. "They dealt me this hand":

♠ QJ6
♡ J3
♢ QJ
♣ AKJ752

"I opened ONE CLUB and partner bid ONE DIAMOND. I rebid TWO CLUBS and he raised to THREE CLUBS. What do you do now?" Marvin glanced at the hand and frowned. He really doesn't like to answer questions. He'd rather hear what action *you* took, and then he'll vigorously agree with you. He gets bigger tips that way. "I guess you would have to make another move," he finally said warily. "Your partner could have the red Aces and the club Queen and three notrump would be a great spot. But you'd be giving your partner perfect cards." "Well," you said, "I felt like I had to bid. It seemed like masterminding not to. So I tried THREE SPADES. That couldn't be a suit, right? I would have bid one spade over one diamond with a spade *suit*." Marvin nodded. "But," you said, "partner could only return to FOUR CLUBS, and I wasn't having any part of an eleven-trick game with all my junk. I quit."

"What happened?" Marvin asked. "Did you go down in four?"

The dummy had turned out to be:

♠ A103
♡ 94
♢ A842
♣ Q963
□
♠ QJ6
♡ J3
♢ QJ
♣ AKJ752

"They cashed two hearts and shifted to a trump," you said as you thrust the hand in front of Marvin on a cocktail napkin. "I won and drew the other trump and took the spade finesse, which lost. They got out with a spade. I took the diamond finesse later and it lost too. So now I'm wondering if I should have passed three clubs after all." (How would you, reader, have played this hand?)

■　　■　　■

The bartender looked at the napkin for another moment. "It just goes to show how little I know about bridge," said Marvin with a smile. "I would have taken the *diamond* finesse first. If it lost, I would have the additional chance that the ten and nine of diamonds would fall on the first three rounds of the suit. Then I would get two diamond pitches for my losing spades. Did somebody actually have 109x or K109 of diamonds?"

"I don't know," you whispered. But you just knew that somebody *had*. They always do when you miss a point of play thanks to taking your eye off the ball for a minute.

"How about a beer, Marvin? No, on second thought, I'll have a martini. Make it a double."

24

Do I have some good news for you! There is a very simple answer to the question of how to be a winner at the bridge table. The answer is, just play up to your capabilities. You definitely do *not* need to produce brilliancies to do well at bridge. You only need to cut the number of easily avoidable errors you make to as near the zero mark as possible. Throughout years of teaching bridge, I've been telling players that anyone with a solid foundation can win in almost any sort of competition. And the best part of an *expert's* game, I think, is that an expert *never* makes a mistake when faced with an elementary problem in bidding or play.

If you don't think that merely avoiding ridiculous results is enough to win at bridge, take a look at this hand. This is from an ACBL tournament, a Sectional Masters' Pairs in fact, where all the players are more or less experienced, if not top echelon:

```
♠ A6
♡ A7
◇ AQ753
♣ K532
        □
♠ K
♡ K642
◇ 104
♣ AQ10976
```

North was dealer and opened ONE DIAMOND at every table I know of. I didn't hear of any madmen who opened one notrump (wrong pattern, plus too many prime values), but I wouldn't bet there weren't any. South responded TWO CLUBS to one diamond, and North raised to FOUR CLUBS, making the value bid. From here, the auctions continued toward slam in different ways, but whenever *North* took over with Blackwood, the good grand slam in clubs was missed. As it happened, South needed to be the one to ask for Aces. He would have been able to visualize a diamond discard on the spade Ace and see the possibility of thirteen tricks. A few pairs, of course, didn't even get to six clubs, languishing in notrump.

There was plenty of room for error in the bidding, but the really sad part of the hand came in the *play* of six clubs. I watched at several tables. One declarer got a spade lead. He discarded his diamond loser on the spade Ace and tried to crossruff for the rest of the tricks. But, as LHO held J84 of trumps, he was overruffed in the end and held to six. Another South decided that her best chance for thirteen tricks was the diamond finesse. But it failed. At a third table, the opening lead was a heart. Declarer won in dummy and started thinking, but, barring some second sight, twelve tricks had become the limit.

The full deal was:

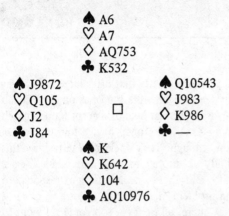

```
              ♠ A6
              ♡ A7
              ◇ AQ753
              ♣ K532
♠ J9872                      ♠ Q10543
♡ Q105                       ♡ J983
◇ J2          □              ◇ K986
♣ J84                        ♣ —
              ♠ K
              ♡ K642
              ◇ 104
              ♣ AQ10976
```

You can see, can't you, that this hand is cold for seven? It's a baby hand,
the kind I'd give to a Beginning Bridge class. A diamond is the only lead to
hold it. Say they lead a heart. Plan the play.

■   ■   ■

Win the heart in hand, saving an entry to the hand most likely to
need one. Play the club Ace. When RHO shows out, get the spade King
out of the way, cross to the diamond Ace, and discard your other diamond on the spade Ace. Ruff a diamond and draw the rest of the trumps,
ending in dummy. Ruff another diamond. Go back to the heart Ace and
ruff another diamond (necessary since diamonds are 4-2), to set up a long
card. Ruff a heart with dummy's last trump, pitch your last heart on the
good diamond, and claim.

Establishing tricks. Counting entries. You can't get much more basic
than that. But six clubs, making thirteen tricks via a simple suit-establishment play, would have been worth *20 matchpoints on a 21 top* in a field
allegedly full of the better class of bridge players.

Maybe there is something strange about this hand, some mysterious
feature that mesmerized all those who played it into dropping a trick. And
then again, maybe it wouldn't hurt for you to go brush up on your basic
technique, especially suit-establishment.

25

In Europe, there are many bridge tournaments that offer large cash prizes to the winners. The various bridge festivals, like the ones on the French Riviera, are popular, and if one wishes, he can play bridge for money much like golfers play the PGA Tour in America. Money bridge tournaments in the U.S. have never caught on, though. It is unclear exactly why this should be so. In 1977, somebody attempted to stage one in Las Vegas, amid great fanfare and publicity. But there was insufficient response to hold the event. One part of the problem might be the spectre of possible cheating. The incentive would be there, all right (or so people are wont to think), and much more so than if mere Master Points were on the line. Another factor is the great difference in ability between the top echelon of professionals and the great mass of average players. There are a limited number of players who would enter a big money event (and maybe pay a stiff entry fee) because they seriously thought they could win it. The main reason for the lack of money tournaments here, however, must be that the ACBL has woven such an influential monopoly on tournament bridge in this country that everybody is conditioned, simply content to play in ACBL tournaments and no others. The only direct reward the League can offer for success in its tournaments is ego gratification, but to many players, that seems to be as eminently satisfying as cold cash.

About the only big money tournament around now is the Cavendish Invitational, run each year by New York's Cavendish Club, traditionally the most prestigious bridge establishment in this country. (With the advent of the new organizations for professional bridge players that the League has approved, there surely will be more attempts to stage money tournaments in the future.)

Playing in the Cavendish Invitational (with IMP-style scoring), you deal yourself this:

♠ 9642
♡ AK62
♢ Q3
♣ 1073

After passes by you and LHO, partner opens ONE DIAMOND. You respond ONE HEART, and partner rebids TWO CLUBS. What do you do now?

■   ■   ■

You are too weak for any forward going action at this point, but it would be very wrong to pass. Partner's change of suit rebid has a fairly wide range, twelve to eighteen high-card points, in Standard American bidding, so game is still possible. A two diamond preference might get you back to your best suit, and it will give partner another chance to bid if he has extra strength. A simple preference to partner's first suit is a weak action, suggesting six to nine high-card points, so partner should not credit you with more than you have simply because you have bid a second time.

Over your TWO DIAMONDS, partner says TWO HEARTS. Should you pass quickly and be done with it?

■   ■   ■

Maybe not. Partner must have an excellent hand to bid a *third* time in the face of your (possibly very) weak preference. His two heart bid says, in effect, that he still thinks game is possible even though he knows you have nine points at most. He would pass with *any* minimum over your two diamonds. So you should bid some more. You should have a game! You try THREE HEARTS, since no other strain looks right on your cards, and partner lifts to FOUR HEARTS.

Your LHO has also been listening to the auction, because expecting dummy to come down with a stiff spade, he leads a trump. You wait to see dummy, hoping you haven't misread partner's intentions.

♠ 10
♡ Q83
♦ AKJ742
♣ AJ5

□

♠ 9642
♡ AK62
♦ Q3
♣ 1073

Partner had a tough rebid over one heart. He hated to rebid three diamonds and make it a little harder to settle into a heart contract. But with only three hearts, he wasn't too excited about raising you directly. His two clubs was a flexible, if uncomfortable, compromise.

The game seems to be a reasonable undertaking. How do you plan the play to protect your Cavendish investment?

■   ■   ■

In any 4-3 fit, you must consider your play carefully. You can try to scramble tricks on a crossruff; try to minimize the danger of the suit the opponents are using to force you out of control; or, if you have lots of side-suit tricks to take (as you do here), you can maneuver to *keep control* of trumps. Your best play here, at least at IMP scoring, is to *duck* the first round of trumps. If the opponents return a second trump, you can draw trumps, assuming a split no worse than 4-2, and run your diamonds for ten tricks. If they shift to spades and force dummy to ruff, you accept the force, cash the heart Queen, come to hand with the diamond Queen, and hope to draw trumps so that you can run the diamonds as before.

You might run into trouble if you fail to duck an early round of trumps; a 4-2 split could spell defeat. Say you win the first trump and play a spade. They win and continue trumps. You win, ruff a spade, and come to the diamond Queen, hoping to draw trumps. They go 4-2. Now if someone can ruff the second diamond, two spade tricks can be cashed against you before you get any discards. You might play the hand this way at matchpoint scoring because the chances of making six are fair and you would be unlucky to go down in four. But at IMPs (or rubber bridge), safest is best, and the early duck of a trump is clearly the safest line.

Maybe next year you should try the European Tour!

26

One of the most widely played conventions in tournament bridge today is Flannery. This is a *two-diamond* opening that promises a minimum hand with four spades and five (or rarely more) hearts! Quaint, don't you think?

There are some problems, which Flannery seeks to overcome, in describing hands of this type. It's a fun gadget to play and I'll bet at least half of the ACBL uses it. For reasons that will be seen, I'm one of the ones who decided to leave it on the shelf.

Now, I cannot deny that there are some advantages to playing Flannery. On some hands, the convention is effective. For instance, it is possible to bid good distributional games that you might miss otherwise. Also, responder does not have to hold his nose and respond one spade to a one heart opening with four to the deuce —opener denied four spades when he opened one heart. If you open one heart with:

♠ AQx
♡ Axxxx
♢ xx
♣ Kxx

and partner says one spade, you can raise in comfort, a desirable action to take at matchpoint scoring. The fact that responder may suppress a four-card spade suit can make the defenders' task a little harder. Your strange two diamond opening can throw the auction into confusion and make it tough for unprepared opponents to compete. And finally, you don't know what true grief is until you open one heart with some 4-5-3-1 pattern, partner responds one notrump (which many pairs happen to play as conventionally forcing), and you try to think of an intelligent second action. All true, all true.

My main gripe against Flannery is that the important factor of suit quality is usually ignored. You can learn about opener's distribution, but it is hard to find out about where his *high cards* are located, and sometimes that matters a lot. There was a hand in the Spring 1982 Charity Game:

Opener	Responder
♠ Axxx	♠ xx
♡ KQ9xx	♡ A10xx
♢ Q10x	♢ Kx
♣ Q	♣ AKJxx

The key to the virtually laydown slam was that magnificent Queen of clubs, solidifying responder's suit. Flannery would have a hard time here. I tend to be suspicious of any convention that turns the auction into an inquisition instead of a dialogue, and that's what Flannery can do. As I said before, though, it's fun to play, so I don't look for my remonstrances to have any great impact.

You were invited over to somebody's house to play DOOP (an interesting one-table home duplicate bridge game). Your partner of the day wanted to play Flannery and it didn't help for you to say you'd never heard of it. He offered to teach it to you and you couldn't turn off his enthusiasm. So, needless to say, the very first board was:

♠ A10853
♡ Q5
♢ AJ74
♣ K10

Partner opened TWO DIAMONDS, beaming. You responded TWO NO-TRUMP, forcing and asking him about his distribution. He bid THREE CLUBS, showing a singleton diamond. Slam chances looked better than just fair, with a stiff diamond opposite your Ace. Partner could have the King-Queen of spades, the heart King, and the club Ace. You thought of bidding *five spades*, which should show worries about the trump suit, but he would go on to six with the Jxxxx of hearts. Hoping to buy some time, you bid THREE SPADES (forcing). He raised to FOUR SPADES, so you were back where you started. Finally, you weaseled with Blackwood. One good convention deserves another. Partner showed one Ace, and you blasted into six spades, hoping for a little good luck.

The opening lead is a club, and this disappointing dummy hits:

♠ Q742
♡ K10742
♢ K
♣ AQ6
　□
♠ A10853
♡ Q5
♢ AJ74
♣ K10

Perhaps partner should have bid three *notrump* over three spades to warn of his poor spades and suggest a singleton diamond *honor*. Or maybe you should have invited slam with five spades, as you thought of doing.

You win the *Queen* of clubs (faking a finesse), and lead a heart. If they let you sneak a heart by, you can discard your other heart on the club. But the heart Ace wins to your left, and you are left only with the chance of picking up the trump suit. Any plans?

■   ■   ■

In a case like this, you just have to be optimistic. Figure out a lie of the cards that will allow you to accomplish your goal, and then play as though that's the way things are. Here, you must assume that LHO has the singleton Jack of trumps. There is no other legitimate way of doing it. Go to dummy and lead the spade Queen. (There is a slight extra chance that a sleepy RHO might forget to cover with Kx, but since this is the first board of the evening, you can't count on his being very sleepy.)

Whatever happens, take time to think of the advantages and disadvantages of Flannery, and consider carefully whether *your* partnership can afford it.

27

When you play bridge at a National Tournament, you can never tell who your opposition will turn out to be. Struggling along in one of the Regionally rated side events, you meet a white-haired but robust man who can be none other than Oswald Jacoby. Carried away with this opportunity, you sneakily get partner to change places with you. You want to occupy the South chair so that it will be easy for Mr. Jacoby to immortalize you in his syndicated column if you do something brilliant. And luck looks to be in your corner (more accurately, on your side of the table) because your first hand is:

♠ A10
♡ J104
♢ KQ53
♣ KQ72

Your one notrump opening starts at sixteen high-card points, so you choose to begin with one of a suit despite the added value of your two tens. In which suit would you open?

■   ■   ■

It's funny how experts can disagree so violently on certain matters of bidding philosophy, even something as simple as choosing an opening bid. In this situation, there would be (loud) supporters for both one club and one diamond. Some writers suggest that the choice between two four-card suits depends on whether the suits are "touching" (in rank). With *non*touching suits, you're supposed to open in the *lower*-ranking suit, but open in the *higher*-ranking with *touching* suits. I have to admit that this scheme has never made much sense to me. The only reason to open in a higher-ranking suit would be to prepare a rebid in the lower-ranking, so that you could show both suits without reversing. But I seldom treat 4–4–3–2 hands as true two-suiters. I would prefer to make my second bid in notrump if possible, as my balanced pattern suggests. Opening one diamond with four cards in each minor would only make a club fit more difficult to uncover, and might land you in some 4–2 diamond fits in a few auctions! I'd never do it unless I desperately wanted a diamond lead, or unless my values were so concentrated in the minors that I was willing to treat my hand like a two-suiter.

Anyway, suppose I impose a ONE CLUB opening on you. Try to cope if you are a confirmed one diamond opener. Partner responds ONE HEART and you rebid ONE NOTRUMP as planned. Partner now raises to TWO NOTRUMP. You have more than enough to accept his invitation, and you do so by bidding THREE HEARTS, offering partner a choice of games. After some thought, he returns to THREE NOTRUMP and you stop.

The opening lead is the spade seven, and the dummy is not totally to your liking:

♠ J642
♡ Q8632
♢ A2
♣ A6
□
♠ A10
♡ J104
♢ KQ53
♣ KQ72

It looks like partner had worries of his own during the auction. He couldn't bid two spades at his second turn; that would have been a *reverse*, and a game force in your methods (and about everybody else's). When you bid three hearts, he decided to play in notrump despite the 5-3 heart fit, apparently because his hearts were so ragged. His decision might be questioned because of his unbalanced pattern (5-4-2-2 hands often play better in a suit) and his primary values in the minors. Even though four hearts may be a superior matchpoint contract, you had better try making three notrump. RHO puts up the spade King at trick one. How do you plan the play?

■   ■   ■

If spades are 4-3, you will make three (maybe four if there is no entry to the long spade). But LHO may well have a five-card suit, from the looks of that seven he led. In that case, they may beat you unless you are careful. Suppose you win the spade Ace and lead a heart. Assuming the heart honors are split, RHO will win the first heart and return his last spade. LHO will establish the suit while he still has an entry.

The correct play to counter this possibility is unusual. You must duck the first trick! They return a spade, but now the opponents' communications are broken up if spades were 5-2 and you will be safe unless *both* heart honors are in the hand with five spades, in which case there is nothing you could have done.

This hand would make a beginner cry. First, he is taught to avoid a hold-up play if it will cost him a trick in the suit. Then he is hit with this hand, on which a hold-up, even though it seems to lose a spade trick, is the right play. Of course, the trick comes back later, and with a little interest. It just goes to show that "always" is a word any aspiring bridge player should be wary of.

When you attack the hearts, by the way, be sure to lead a *low* one from your hand, and not an honor, just in case LHO has the singleton Ace or King.

(Scary postscript: If RHO has KQ98 of spades on this hand, with LHO having led the spade seven from three small, you will make the Jacoby column all right, but you may not enjoy reading about yourself.)

28

Just mention the words "grand slam" and you won't find very many bridge players who won't get a wistful gleam in their eyes, with a trace of awe and terror mixed in. The sound of distant trumpets may be faintly heard, and players will probably lose no time in telling you about the time they won a crucial match or a pile of money by bringing home a grand on the last board of the evening.

On the other side of the coin, the late Hal Sims used to castigate his teammates anytime they bid seven, even if they made it! Sims thought that grand slams were chancy propositions, because they could always be beaten by an unexpected ruff at trick one. He figured that, in a match against a weaker team, the only way he could lose would be to bid a grand slam and get set.

Perhaps Sims was familiar with the *odds* on bidding grand slams. At rubber bridge, the odds are against going to seven unless your chances of making rate to be considerably better than average. If you go down in seven, you lose not only the small slam bonus you would have earned by stopping in six, but also the *game* bonus. So you have more to lose than you have to gain. At IMP scoring, the situation is about the same: you will lose more IMPs by going down in seven while six is bid and made at the other table than you stand to pick up if you make the grand. (Strangely, there are plenty of times when a grand slam is bid at one table and at the other table they stop in *game*. Here, any grand slam risks losing a great many IMPs to gain very few.)

At matchpoints, you should seldom bid a grand slam unless it is especially obvious and you can practically count thirteen tricks in the bidding. Very few pairs in a typically weak matchpoint field will bid seven unless this is the case, so you have a lot to lose by speculating. Remember that, if there is anything to the play and thirteen tricks are difficult to manage or depend on the opening lead, you will get a good score for making seven whether you bid that many or not.

Keeping all that in mind, take a look at this hand, Playing matchpoints against a pair you don't like, you would like nothing better than to saddle them with a resounding bottom. So as if to tempt you, fate passes out:

♠ AQ6
♡ AJ10852
♦ AK10
♣ K

Judging that you aren't quite strong enough to insist on game, you open ONE HEART. And partner delights you by responding THREE HEARTS. As you play, this is a *limit raise*, showing invitational values and good trump support. Wheeling out "Old Black" looks reasonable at this point. If partner can show an Ace and two Kings, you can bid seven hearts with great expectations. Partner shows one Ace over your FOUR NOTRUMP all right, but when you continue with FIVE NOTRUMP to ask for Kings, he can only admit to one. What now? Do you still entertain fond thoughts of seven?

■　　■　　■

The temptation is great all right, and the chance for a glorious victory is inclined to cloud your judgment. Maybe partner has the AQx of clubs or the QJxxx of diamonds, and you will make it. Perhaps seven will only depend on a finesse at worst. Eventually, cupidity gets the best of you. "SEVEN HEARTS"! All pass. A small club is led, and you await the appearance of dummy with a gnawing doubt.

♠ 9754
♡ KQ93
◇ 854
♣ AJ
☐
♠ AQ6
♡ AJ10852
◇ AK10
♣ K

No doubt you were entirely too greedy. The problem was, you were giving partner specific cards, and somehow, he never seems to have them. He always has one of the million other hands that make slam a precarious venture. You could even have been off the King of trumps here, which would make any grand slam totally undesirable. But try to forget the bidding for now. How do you plan to make this hand?

■   ■   ■

The spade finesse will be necessary for starters. Assuming that it works, you will still need another spade trick or the double finesse in diamonds. To take advantage of all your chances will require a little care. Win the club King, play a middle trump to dummy, and lead a spade to your Queen. (Mumble a prayer if you know any.) When the Queen holds, cash the spade Ace and play another middle trump to dummy, discard your last spade on the club Ace, and ruff a spade high. If the suit splits 3-3, you can cross to dummy with a trump and cash the thirteenth spade for a diamond discard.

If spades fail to come in, you must be able to get back to the dummy *twice* so as to take two diamond finesses. If you have saved two trumps in dummy and have preserved the deuce in your hand, the two entries you need will be available.

Your chances of making your grand slam will be about one in four, and if thirteen tricks do materialize, allow me to offer you a little friendly advice: next time, stop in six.

29

Now that the Age of the Computer has emerged in full bloom, it was inevitable that somebody would come out with a machine that purports to play bridge. But since bridge is a game of almost infinite variety and complexity, the bridge playing computers are no threat to win any championships for the moment. I've played with some of the models currently on the market. They seem limited in their technical scope, and, of course, they fail to display anything at all in the way of creativity or imagination.

By the time you read this book, there will probably be newer, more advanced models available. It is obvious that, with the incredible progress in computer technology made over the past decade, we are rapidly moving closer to a bridge playing computer that will be able to compete with a real live player, at least on a technical basis. But that brings up another question. Will any machine ever be able to assimilate the personal and psychological aspects of the game? Will it know how to placate partner, or deliver a withering blast at his ineptitudes? Or how to play the opponents to best advantage? Could a silicon chip ever be made to play this deal . . . ?

Playing in a Regional on the East Coast, you sit down against two fat ladies. For some reason, fat ladies always seem to be in *ample* supply at bridge tournaments. Once I went to a Regional, and the entire field seemed to be fat ladies, stretching as far as the eye could see. I don't know whether it's just that fat ladies have lots of time to play bridge, or that bridge and lots of it is conducive to a little healthy plumpness. The fat ladies are generally very nice. They just all look the same.

Anyway it's you and partner vs. the fat ladies. The fat lady on your right is dealer. She takes her cards out of the board, looks them over carefully, checks the vulnerability, reexamines her cards, frowns, and passes. You are next to speak, with:

♠ AK1052
♡ AJ6
♦ 63
♣ J103

You open ONE SPADE and partner responds TWO NOTRUMP. In your system, that shows a *forcing raise* in spades. Since you want to play *limit* double raises, you have to find some other way to describe a forcing raise. So you adopt one of Mr. Jacoby's innovations. Over two notrump, you have the option of bidding three of a new suit to show a *singleton* there; four of a new suit to show a big two-suiter with slam interest (or a void, if you prefer); or three spades or three notrump to suggest more balanced slam tries. With your actual hand, you hastily sign off at FOUR SPADES. This Jacoby Two notrump response is a useful and effective convention. All you give up to use it is a natural two notrump response, not a serious or irreplaceable loss.

The opening lead against four spades is the diamond Jack, and you see:

♠ Q963
♡ K104
♢ K84
♣ AQ6
☐
♠ AK1052
♡ AJ6
♢ 63
♣ J103

Prospects look reasonable. The Jack of diamonds holds the first trick. LHO continues with a low diamond to RHO's Queen. RHO then tries to cash the diamond Ace, and you ruff. Having no reason not to do so, you draw trumps, taking care to play a high one from your own hand first, in case there is a 4-0 split. The trumps turn out to be 2-2 though, with RHO having Jx. With the trumps in, you take the club finesse, which loses. And RHO returns a club, leaving you to figure out the heart situation for yourself. Who do you play for the Queen?

■   ■   ■

A bidding chart impassively shows the bids that were made in the auction and doesn't include such things as hesitations, vocal inflections, and so forth. But the expert declarer listens to *everything* that happens in the bidding, and makes use of whatever extraneous things occur if he thinks they are legitimate indications to point his way. RHO hitched before passing as dealer. The hitch seemed to be connected with her hand. She wasn't just daydreaming when she failed to pass promptly, or thinking about where her next box of candy was coming from. Up to this point, RHO has showed 10 high-card points in the play (diamond Ace-Queen, club King, spade Jack). With no other high cards, would she have had any problem passing as dealer? You doubt it. But with the heart Queen in addition, she would have had a borderline opening, and, for an instant, might have been tempted to open. A hand like:

♠ Jx
♡ Qxxx
♢ AQxx
♣ Kxx

is the kind that often produces the good old "twelve-point twitch" in less experienced players.

If and when the computers take over, hands like this will go the way of all flesh. Somehow, I can't imagine a mechanical opponent twitching. So you had better learn to draw inferences from what goes on at the table while you still can.

30

Playing at the club, you find yourself at the same table with *three* of your pupils. It wouldn't be a good time for you to have any accidents. Your reputation would be sullied forever. On the first board of the round you are dummy, which might be the best part of your game anyway. But things are different on the second board. You are second hand, with:

♠ A63
♡ QJ1074
♢ KQJ
♣ 94

After a pass on your right, you open ONE HEART. Partner thinks for a while and responds TWO CLUBS. You decide to rebid TWO HEARTS instead of two notrump because you have no tenaces, and no help for the clubs at notrump. Partner raises to THREE HEARTS. Would you go on?

■   ■   ■

The decision you must make is a close one. You have seven losers. Could partner cover four of them? It's not impossible at all. The heart King, club Ace and King, and a little shape would do it, and partner could have an additional value like the club Jack which would give you an extra chance. Also, against the present opposition, you probably won't get a devastating defense. So you decide to shoot it out in FOUR HEARTS.

All pass, the Jack of spades hits the table on your left, and partner puts down the dummy complaining that she didn't know what to do.

♠ K84
♡ A962
♢ 74
♣ KJ102
□
♠ A63
♡ QJ1074
♢ KQJ
♣ 94

Partner had to temporize with that two club response because no immediate heart raise was exactly right. (Even if you are playing *limit raises*, and an immediate double raise is invitational, not forcing, you would do better to suppress your support temporarily and show a side suit if you have values concentrated there. Partner may be able to judge the hand's potential a little more accurately if he knows where your side strength is. The inability to bid your side suit on hands with invitational strength is a possible flaw of bidding systems in which a two-over-one response is *forcing to game*.)

Meanwhile, your chances of going down in four hearts are quite good. You are off one or two clubs, a sure diamond, a possible trump, and a spade. Plan your play.

■   ■   ■

Your spade loser will go on a high diamond in your hand, and then you will need the trump finesse or a good guess in clubs.

If you want to get careless and make a fatal error, I can't think of a better way than to play to the first trick and *then* start thinking about the rest of the hand. Hasty play to the first trick may be the single most common error perpetrated in declarer play. Having thought everything over carefully, you win the first trick in dummy and lead a diamond. Any trump play would be premature. If you took a losing trump finesse at trick two, the opponents would get a chance to lead spades again, setting up their trick in that suit before you get your diamond discard available. You would have "lost a tempo," and would be down at least one.

As it is, your Jack of diamonds wins the second trick, and you continue with the King, won on your right. A spade comes back, and you are able to win in your own hand this time, as you planned earlier, so that you can immediately discard dummy's spade loser on the diamond Queen. One loser away.

Now you can play trumps. The heart Queen loses to RHO, though, and a trump is returned. LHO shows out. You ruff your last spade with the trump Ace and return a low heart to your hand, drawing the last trump. Now you have to guess clubs for the contract. LHO plays low when you lead a club toward dummy. What is your guess?

■　　■　　■

This is as easy as pie if you pay attention to all the available information. RHO passed as dealer, and is known to have had at least nine high-card points (spade Queen, heart King, diamond Ace). So the club Ace has to be on your left. If RHO had it, she would have opened the bidding.

Surprisingly, your four hearts making four is worth a cold top on this board, and your pupils are suitably impressed. "How did you do that?" one of them asks. "I just made a lucky guess," you say with a smile. One day soon you can explain to them all about your thought processes on this deal. But for the time being, why not let them continue to think your're a magician with a handy crystal ball?

31

At a typical Nationals, many events are running concurrently. There are the National Championships, which attract the strongest fields and carry the most prestige. There are Regionally rated events every day. And, for those with nothing better to do, there are the one-session side games. A strange conglomeration of players is found in the side games: nationally known pairs tuning up for the big one the next day; old friends playing together; new partnerships being tried out; and the usual crop of little old ladies and rank beginners. At least as many interesting hands are produced here as come out of the better known events. And the game itself is somewhat affectionately known as the "Side Show."

You arrived at the tournament just in time for the evening session. You could kibitz, of course, but why do that when you can play in the side game? Early in the session, you pick up:

♠ AK7532
♡ 74
◊ A9
♣ KQ6

With your side vulnerable, partner opens ONE CLUB and there is a ONE HEART overcall. Think over carefully how you would plan the auction.

■ ⬛ ■

Suppose you bid one spade only. Partner will probably make some minimum rebid, like one notrump. What would you do then? Even if you can now bid a *forcing* three spades or three clubs (and most pairs play that a jump preference or jump rebid here is merely invitational), you will feel like you still haven't done enough if partner just bids three notrump. Surely it is better to go ahead and show your *slam* interest with a jump shift immediately instead of trying to catch up later. Over your TWO SPADES, partner bids TWO NOTRUMP as you half expect. Now you try THREE CLUBS. If partner bids three notrump in *this* sequence, you can quit with a clear conscience. But partner bids THREE HEARTS. You cue-bid FOUR DIAMONDS, and partner thinks it over and takes the plunge to SIX

CLUBS. (Some players might like a little better club fit, e.g., a fourth club, to bid as you have, but I think the alternatives to a jump shift are worse on this hand.)

Your partner suddenly receives an emergency phone call, and, by special dispensation, you are allowed to play the dummy for him. So you can move around the table and try to make this slam. The diamond King is opened, and you see:

♠ AK7532
♡ 74
◇ A9
♣ KQ6
□
♠ 104
♡ AKJ3
◇ 63
♣ A10742

This is a fair slam, even after a diamond opening KOs dummy's entry. Your chances of reaching it without an immediate jump shift would not be good. How should you plan the play?

■   ■   ■

To have a chance, you will have to set up spades. You cannot try to ruff hearts in dummy, since RHO will surely overruff. The spades will have to split 3-2 for you; you don't have the entries to cope with a 4-1 split (after drawing trumps, that is; and if you don't draw trumps, they will ruff one of your high spades). Don't be surprised if you go down. LHO overcalled on a bad suit, so he may have good distribution to make up for it.

You win the diamond Ace, cash one top spade, and lead a club to your Ace. You might make this against some 4-1 club splits if you keep two club entries in dummy. Next, you lead your other spade toward dummy. If LHO ruffs this, you will be down, but at least you get to *save* your other high spade and you can probably avoid being set two or three. Both opponents follow to the second spade. So far, so good. Now you continue with a third round of spades. If RHO follows again, you plan to discard your losing diamond. (If you were to ruff, they might overruff and cash a diamond.). But RHO pitches a heart on the third spade, and you ruff. When you lead a club to dummy, LHO shows out, which is OK. You just start running your good spades through RHO. If he ruffs in with his club Jack, you discard your losing diamond, and make the rest easily. If he refuses to ruff, you discard all your losers, and can claim all but one after cashing the last high trump in dummy. Making six on this borderline slam hand should earn you a fine score, especially in the side show.

There used to be a popular myth that responder needed "19 points" to jump shift. But if you have a nineteen-point hand, you will usually bid a slam come what may, and it matters little whether you start proceedings wih a jump shift or go slowly. A jump shift will prove most effective when you want to *suggest the possibility* of slam to partner and elicit his cooperation if he also senses there might be one. I recommend you jump shift *whenever you can visualize a slam opposite some suitable minimum in your partner's hand* (and you have a good idea in what *strain* the slam will be bid). Often, a jump shift *to begin with* will save you some unpleasant guessing later in the auction, and may even keep you lower in the long run.

32

There are times when the character of a person can be revealed over a bridge game. The truth may come out of hiding. Thankfully, there are opportunities for the display of many virtues at the bridge table, virtues such as modesty, honesty, and a good sense of humor; and the majority of players you will meet are very pleasant, away from the table as well as otherwise. However, there are always a few bad apples in any barrel. At bridge, the bad apples are the ones who can't shake off a lurking feeling of inadequacy. To compensate, they are inclined to berate their partner and/or the opponents and belittle their efforts. All sorts of players, good and bad, are susceptible to this disease, which indicates what an ego trip bridge really is for everybody. And not many of these players are willing to face up to the problem and try to keep from being nasty. I don't know many players who really strive for bad feeling at the table. The tension it can cause can keep you from concentrating and playing your best. Moreover, my experience suggests that it's a whole lot easier to beat somebody who *likes* you than somebody who wants to send you home in a box. So I'd try staying on good terms with the world if I were you.

Playing in a Regional Masters' Pairs, your LHO advertised his bad manners on the first board by making some derogatory comments about your partner's declarer play. Comes the second board, and you hold:

♠ A5
♡ Q7
♢ K942
♣ A10842

They are vulnerable. LHO snarls ONE HEART, and your partner DOUBLES defiantly. There should be a game for your side somewhere, but *which* game is the question. So you begin with a TWO HEART cue-bid, informing partner that you have a good hand, and want to look around for a spot to play in. The opponents stay out and your partner says *THREE* HEARTS. Apparently, he has extra strength and wants *you* to suggest a suit. You try FOUR CLUBS, and partner bids FOUR SPADES. Could that be a suit? Surely not a good one—he would have bid spades earlier, or should have, at any rate. Sweating a little now, you decide to bid FOUR NOTRUMP. Perhaps partner will interpret that as asking for a choice of the minors, but if the turkey thinks it's Ace-asking, you may still get out of this alive. Over four notrump, partner goes into a long tank, while you feel a prickly sensation starting to invade your scalp. Finally, he smiles, puts his cards on the table, and says firmly, "I pass."

Now be careful. Partner has almost surely made a horrendous error, but you can always explain that to him *after* the session. For now, you simply have to keep your composure. The slightest break in your facade and the opponents will know that the contract is disastrous. So smile and try to look happy about the situation for as long as you can.

LHO bangs down the heart King, and the end of the world is seen on the table. You are sorely tempted to offer partner a few choice comments of your own:

♠ Q10642
♡ 5
♢ AQ63
♣ KQ5
□
♠ A5
♡ Q7
♢ K942
♣ A10842

Not the best contract you've ever been in, perhaps. Partner's bidding is just dreadful, and not just the pass to four notrump. His takeout double (instead of a one spade overcall) stood to lose a possible 5-3 spade fit, since he certainly cannot double and then bid spades himself. His three hearts was ill-considered, since cue-bidding should be postponed until a suit is mentioned and a fit is found.

As for the four notrump contract; well, if they beat you, they beat you. But don't let it be because you gave away the fact that the contract is hopeless. On the contrary, you should exude satisfaction and confidence! After LHO wins the first trick, he starts thinking, which should make you feel a little better. Eventually, he shifts to a diamond! He thinks that a heart continuation will set up your Queen for a possibly vital trick. RHO plays the diamond ten, and you win. You play a diamond to dummy hopefully, but RHO discards a low spade. Where do you go from here?

■　　■　　■

You have only nine top tricks, but five rounds of clubs should improve your position. LHO has the diamond guard, the spade King, and the heart Ace, and may have some problems saving everything. Clubs turn out to be 4-1, with RHO having Jxxx; so LHO has to find four pitches on the clubs. He cannot throw a diamond, so he lets go of a spade and three hearts, looking more and more uncomfortable. With five cards to play, you know he is down to two diamonds and three major-suit cards. Just cash the spade Ace. If the King fails to drop, LHO must still have it. So you continue with another spade and LHO wins. He will have only the heart Ace left to cash, and then he will have to lead to dummy. (There are other lines to make the contract as well.)

After the play, with four notrump having been made, your LHO makes some comment (rude, but justified) about the insanity of your partner's bidding. At this point, nobody has yet realized that your heart stopper was nonexistent. You can't stand it and you break your own personal rule. "You know," you say to LHO with a leer, "you could have set me a million if you had just played that other top heart." The eyebrows arch on your left. "And," you finish up, "I'm really quite surprised you didn't, an obvious expert like yourself."

33

There are many candidates for the worst headache in modern tournament bridge: rude bridge players; increasing costs to go to tournaments; too many Life Masters; and a few others. But my vote goes without hesitation to the cigarette smoke. I can come home from a tournament or even from a session at the local club duplicate, and my wife has no trouble identifying where I've been from the smell of my clothes. The smell pervades the atmosphere at tournaments. A thin layer of haze is sometimes seen hovering over the playing area.

The ACBL recognizes the problem and has offered partial remedies by providing sections for nonsmokers and even separate Smoking and Nonsmoking events at many of its tournaments. In a very few places, there is a total ban on smoking. Nevertheless, much of the time I want to play tournament bridge, I'm still forced to breathe unclean air to do it. Not long ago, I had a conversation with one of the leading American woman players. "I had a physical exam last year," she told me. "I've never smoked, but the doctor swore I was a smoker from the looks of the X-rays he took of my lungs. That's what has happened to me from playing so much bridge." I was genuinely disturbed by this comment. It points up a problem the League will have to face head on sooner or later.*

Playing in a Sectional Open Pairs (no nonsmoking sections available), you arrive at a table where the haze is particularly thick. The opponents, both of them chomping on big black cigars, are seen only as dim silhouettes through the gloom. You manage to find your chair, locate the board, and take out your cards. A voice on your left says pass, and two more passes follow from somewhere nearby.

Your hand is:

♠ 64
♡ KQ106542
♢ K42
♣ K

*Regulations adopted by the ACBL Board of Directors in July, 1983 should improve the situation somewhat.

You must surely open, since there could very easily be a game your way. But you would like to make it hard for the opponents to compete as well. This is not a classic weak two bid, but with partner a passed hand, you can afford to deceive him a little. Your TWO HEART opening is passed out, much to your satisfaction.

The Queen of diamonds is led, and the table hits with a suitable hand:

♠ KJ1053
♡ A7
◇ 7
♣ Q9653
□
♠ 64
♡ KQ106542
◇ K42
♣ K

RHO wins the diamond Ace, and fires back the trump three. How do you plan the play?

■　　■　　■

You want to make *ten* tricks to get a good score, and the simplest approach is to establish a club pitch for your losing diamond and then try to guess the spades. Should you not try instead to ruff a diamond in dummy? No, it's impractical. You cannot win the trump switch in your hand and ruff a diamond with the trump Ace; you would lose a trump trick then if someone had Jxx of trumps to begin with. And if you win the second trick with dummy's trump *Ace*, saving the low one, you cannot get off dummy without letting the opponents in to play a second trump. Anyway, the spade guess may not prove too difficult.

You win the second trick in hand, saving the heart Ace as an entry, and lead the club King. LHO wins the Ace and continues the Jack of trumps to dummy, RHO following. You discard your little diamond on the club Queen, as LHO follows with the ten, and ruff a club to hand. LHO shows out, discarding a diamond. Now you lead a spade toward dummy. Low on your left. How would you guess it?

■　　■　　■

Not much of a guess, really, as we surmised. LHO is a passed hand and has showed the diamond Queen-Jack, the club Ace, and the heart Jack, along with some probable diamond length. With the spade Ace in addition to those values, he would have opened the bidding or competed. So you play dummy's ten of spades, and make your four when RHO has to produce the Ace.

Plus 170 on this board turned out to be a good score, since almost nobody got to game, and quite a few declarers mismanaged the play in one way or another. The best thing about the round, though, was that the second board was passed out, so you got to get up and go outside for some fresh air.

34

My next-door neighbor owns a large basset hound. Some intro for a bridge hand, right? The beast is a typical basset hound, with the huge, drooping ears and the perpetually sad expression, as if it fully expects some woeful event to occur in the next minute.

It occurred to me that Basil (that's the hound) and the bridge expert have a lot in common. The expert is just as gloomy in his own way as the dog. He operates under Murphy's Law, which confidently states that if anything can go wrong, it will. He knows full well that he is the unluckiest bridge player in the whole wide world, having met a variety of misfortunes in his long career. And so, he approaches the play of every hand with deliberate care, alert for the small detail that might be a potential pitfall if overlooked. It is the mark of a fine declarer that he treats the routine hands with just as much care as the difficult ones, so that he never messes up a hand that should be laydown.

Your club planned to hold a "Pro-Am" and you were asked to play. This is a fun event that some clubs run occasionally as a promotion to boost attendance and encourage the new players. All the experienced players consent to be paired up with a novice. Luckily, they wanted you to be one of the experts, not one of the beginners. So here you are with a wide eyed partner across the table who expects a miracle every time you make a bid or play.

After a while, this hand comes along. You deal and hold:

♠ A6
♡ KQ10853
♢ AKJ63
♣ —

What is your action?

■   ■   ■

You have, in theory, enough winners and defensive values to open two clubs (or two hearts if you prefer strong two-bids). But with this two-suiter, it might be wise to start bidding your suits right away in case the auction gets crowded with competition. A one heart opening is unlikely to get passed out when you have this much shape and only seventeen high-card points. Over your ONE HEART, LHO overcalls ONE SPADE, and partner raises to TWO HEARTS. Since the right minimum in partner's hand could easily produce a slam (even a grand), you must make a slam move. What should you bid?

■   ■   ■

Four diamonds is probably your best bid. This must show slam interest, since you would just bid four hearts if your aspirations were limited to game; and it suggests a big red two-suiter. Partner should cooperate with good trumps, plus help in diamonds or a side Ace. Some players might bid only three diamonds with your cards, but partner could not know that you were interested in *slam* if you made that bid and also might think that you needed more help from him in diamonds. A two spade cue-bid is also unlikely to accomplish much. Partner might not work out your intentions.

Over your FOUR DIAMONDS, you hear FIVE CLUBS by partner. So you have a place to put your spade loser, and partner should have decent trumps and a little diamond help. So you leap to SIX HEARTS, expecting that contract to have a good play.

LHO leads the spade Queen, and a powerful dummy hits:

♠ K853
♡ J94
◇ Q5
♣ A853

□

♠ A6
♡ KQ10853
◇ AKJ63
♣ —

You can see that partner's two hearts was a slight underbid, with the spade King improved because of the overcall. But partner did well to raise your hearts instead of bidding notrump, which probably would have made slam harder to reach. It looks like you have reached a laydown contract. Just draw trumps and ... wait a minute. You know what I said about easy hands. And you are supposed to be the expert here. How do you play?

■   ■   ■

The danger is fairly obvious, and only carelessness can beat your slam. If LHO has six spades and the trump Ace, he will let RHO ruff your second spade winner when he wins his trump. You appear to be solid for tricks anyway, so there is no reason not to win the first trick in dummy and discard the spade Ace on the club Ace, avoiding the possible ruff.

When you next lead the nine of hearts, LHO wins and forces you with a spade (RHO shows out, sure enough). You ruff and take another round of trumps, finding that RHO had three to start with. Now, just a little more care. Test diamonds before you draw the last trump. If LHO had a hand like:

♠ QJ10xxx
♡ A
◇ x
♣ Q10xxx

you will be able to ruff your losing diamond in dummy as RHO has to follow suit.

35

Practicing in the Saturday night game for a Regional the next weekend, you pick up this nondescript collection:

♠ K742
♡ J73
♢ AKJ
♣ A104

Your opening bid is ONE NOTRUMP, and partner replies TWO CLUBS. RHO comes in with TWO HEARTS. It looks as if partner may have spades, so you go ahead and bid TWO SPADES instead of passing the interference around to see if he wants to double. He puts you in FOUR SPADES, and nobody has anything else to say.

A low heart is led against you, and the dummy looks promising:

♠ A853
♡ 8
♢ Q64
♣ K9852
　　□
♠ K742
♡ J73
♢ AKJ
♣ A104

If the trumps don't doublecross you and go 4-1 or worse, you will make at least four. They win the heart with the Queen on your right, and switch to a small diamond. You win in hand, ruff a heart, and lead a club off dummy. RHO plays the Jack, and you win. You ruff another heart, LHO following. Now you try the spade Ace and King, and to your relief, both opponents follow suit. So you proceed to cash your diamond winners, and the opponents each politely play diamonds. The position is now:

♠ —
♡ —
◇ —
♣ K985
　□
♠ 74
♡ —
◇ —
♣ 104

Where do you go from here. Any thoughts about your play for a crucial overtrick?

■　　■　　■

No problem for the moment. Lead a trump and concede them their trick. As it happens, RHO wins the third spade and forces you to ruff a heart. LHO shows out on this trick, pitching the thirteenth diamond. Can you work it out now? You can if you can count to thirteen. RHO had six hearts, three diamonds, three trumps. That Jack of clubs was a singleton. So you lead a club to dummy's nine. It'll win unless you are playing with a strange deck.

One overtrick should be worth some matchpoints in the Saturday night game!

part two

NOT SO EASY

In the usual cut-in rubber bridge game, it is said, time is money. The primary objective, at least for the stronger players, is to get as many hands played as possible, so that whatever technical edge they posses will have adequate opportunity to assert itself. (At bridge, the better player's edge is *less* than it would be in other games, like poker, to mention probably the best example.) So the bidding can often be rather slapdash, with science tossed to the winds in favor of expediency.

Playing in a game such as this, with the stakes astronomical, you pick up:

♠ Q53
♡ A3
◇ KJ53
♣ AQ103

Your partner opens ONE SPADE. There are many possible approaches for you, most of them time consuming and not guaranteed to get you anywhere. Your partner doesn't look overly intelligent anyway, so you give up on any beautiful, delicate sequences to get to six of a minor on a 4-3 fit, and blast into THREE NOTRUMP. Maybe partner will still bid something if there is a slam.

All pass, and the opening lead is the heart six, revealing:

♠ AK1084
♡ J8
◇ A962
♣ J6

□

♠ Q53
♡ A3
◇ KJ53
♣ AQ103

Too bad. Six diamonds looks awfully tasty. Perhaps you should have taken your chances with a two club response, despite partner's dull expression, and looked around a little for the best contract. Technically, the response of three notrump to an opening suit bid should be used only with a completely square hand that offers little prospect of playing in a suit.

There is still three notrump to be made, don't forget. How do you plan the play?

■   ■   ■

To begin with, try the Jack of hearts. Maybe LHO led from a suit headed by the King-Queen. The Queen covers on your right. You win immediately, since a holdup is most unlikely to help you, and it would only tell the opponents they have made a promising start on defense. Next, lay down the Queen of spades. If spades are 3-2, you are cold; and you can handle J9xx on your left; but if the suit happens to be 5-0, with the length on your left, you have to play the spade Queen first to retain your chance for five tricks. All follow to the Queen of spades, but LHO discards a club on the next round. So much for spades. What can you try next?

■   ■   ■

Try the diamonds. If the Queen falls doubleton, you have nine tricks. And, since you do *not* plan to finesse in diamonds, you will cash the diamond King first. This will let you make four diamond tricks if the Queen happens to be singleton on your right. Both opponents follow to the high diamonds, but no Queen appears. Things are getting desperate. You have only one chance left out of the many you started with. You take the club finesse, and, finally, a little justice. It works, and you make three notrump on the nose, panting.

The play of many hands, as you can see from this one, consists of combining as many chances as possible to make the contract. Two or three or four chances are better than just one. Your chances of making three notrump on this deal, assuming you avail yourself of every possibility, add up to better than 95 percent.

37

If you can find some way to win your last match in the Swiss Teams, you will finish somewhere in the overall rankings, and pick up a few of those precious Gold Points. The first board out gives you a chance to establish an advantage (or a disadvantage).

With no one vulnerable, you look at:

♠ K5
♡ KJ53
♢ AKJ
♣ KJ74

You open ONE CLUB. The opponents remain silent as partner responds ONE SPADE, and you rebid TWO NOTRUMP. Partner now expresses his doubts about notrump with THREE CLUBS, but you seem to have the red suits pretty well tied up, so you go ahead and bid THREE NOTRUMP anyway.

Partner shrugs and passes, LHO puts down the seven of hearts, and you see this dummy:

♠ AQ63
♡ 2
♢ 853
♣ Q10852
□
♠ K5
♡ KJ53
♢ AKJ
♣ KJ74

RHO plays the heart Queen at trick one, and you have a crucial decision to make right away. What are your thoughts?

■   ■   ■

If LHO has the club Ace, you are safe to go ahead and win right away. But if RHO has it, what you have to do is *duck* the first trick, and duck again if a heart is returned. By waiting to take your sure heart trick, you could exhaust RHO of his hearts and make it impossible for the defenders to run the whole suit against you.

This is pretty much a straight guess, and *either* line of play could turn out to be the winner. However, guessing well in these situations is one attribute of a fine declarer, and there is the barest whisper of an inference here on which a good player might decide to base his play. If LHO had five or six good hearts and the club Ace (and, don't forget, somebody holds the Queen of diamonds as well), he might have overcalled your one club opening with one heart. Since he did not do this, there is slightly more of a case for *holding up* in hearts.

38

In one of his more famous illustrations, the cartoonist Webster depicted two seedy, down and out hoboes commiserating with each other on a park bench. One sadly admits he didn't draw his trumps, while the other says ruefully that he drew trumps instead of using 'em to ruff his losers.

Are there, as the legends tell us, really men out there walking the streets because they neglected to draw trumps? (I've never met any, but that doesn't mean they don't exist. Perhaps they are ghosts, condemned to an existence in limbo for their trump suit transgressions.) I'm sure that if there *are* such pitiful creatures as these, there must be a lot *more* who wander around because they drew trumps *too soon*.

There are times, you know, when the drawing of trumps must be postponed. Declarer may need to use some of dummy's trumps for ruffing, he may need transportation which only the trump suit can provide, he may have to develop his side suit early to keep control of the play, or he may have timing problems (with something more important to do first). There are other situations as well that demand care in drawing trumps. Here is one that is not so obvious.

You are playing in a Mens' Pairs, a tough event, and you are opposed by the number one seed in your section. The opponents, therefore, won't be giving much away. You are the dealer, with:

♠ K74
♡ A
◇ AKQJ863
♣ 53

You open ONE DIAMOND. The opponents remain silent as partner responds TWO CLUBS. There is a case for you to leap to three notrump now. Three notrump might be the best contract, especially at matchpoint scoring, and partner might not be able to bid it if you make the pedestrian three diamond rebid. He might, for example, be looking at:

♠ xx
♡ Qxx
◇ xx
♣ AKJxxx

However, your slam chances seem reasonable, and that argues against any masterminding. You decide to be straight down the middle. Partner will not pass your THREE DIAMONDS (your jump rebid promises sixteen points at least, and he is known to have no less than ten for his response in a new suit at the two level), and you may get to learn more about his hand from his next bid. He raises to FOUR DIAMONDS. He must have some useful stuff to suggest an eleven-trick contract. With your controls in both major suits, you might as well wheel out Blackwood now. Partner shows one Ace and you bid SIX DIAMONDS. Not a very delicate auction, but maybe there will be some chance to make the slam.

The opening lead is the heart Jack, and you see right away that part-ner has very little to spare:

♠ Q8
♡ Q83
◊ 1095
♣ AQJ106
□
♠ K74
♡ A
◊ AKQJ863
♣ 53

Perhaps partner should have taken a shot at three notrump over three dia-monds, with his lack of prime values and his major-suit tenaces. (Yes, a Qx can be a tenace, opposite Axx or Kxx.) Or, maybe you should have fol-lowed your instincts and shot three notrump on your cards. But for the moment, what about six diamonds? It looks as though the contract de-pends strictly on the club finesse, doesn't it? Can you see any way to im-prove your chances?

■　　■　　■

For openers, you *cover* the Jack of hearts with dummy's Queen. This may create a desirable illusion when the King covers and you win your Ace. There will be a powerful suggestion that you have a low heart in hand and tried to win the first trick without spending your Ace. If the club finesse loses, the opponents may try to cash a heart trick instead of their Ace of spades.

The other thing you can do here—and this goes back to our original theme—is to take the club finesse at trick *two*. The trouble with drawing trumps first is that LHO may get a chance to discard a high spade, showing possession of the Ace, and making the defenders' task a lot easier. (They will know you do not have a spade *void* because you used Blackwood; that would be ill-advised with a void suit.)

39

A vital part of competitive bidding, especially at matchpoint duplicate, is "balancing." When the opponents stop bidding at a low level, and especially when they have found a fit, you should consider backing into the auction, even though you weren't strong enough to take any direct action previously. Your side is marked with a substantial share of the high cards in this situation, and the fact that the opponents have located a trump suit makes it likely that your side has one as well. It is losing tactics, at any form of scoring, to let the opponents play peacefully right where they want to at the one or two level. If you "balance" with a bid or a (takeout) double, you may get your side to a makable contract, or drive the opponents to a higher level where you will have a better chance to set them.

Playing in the Turkeyville Sectional, you pick up:

♠ KQ1063
♡ AJ3
♦ Q8
♣ Q74

ONE CLUB is opened on your left (the opponents play Standard American), and this is followed by two passes. With this much strength, you decide to DOUBLE, planning to bid spades at your next turn. The trouble with overcalling one spade is that you might do that with a *lot* less in this situation. You would balance with an overcall on a seven-point hand. If you double and then bid here, you suggest that you have a sound hand and were not just balancing with a weakish one.

Over your double, partner bids ONE HEART, and you proceed with ONE SPADE. Partner now raises you to FOUR SPADES! Oops. Maybe he thinks you have some great big hand. Pairs often have trouble with balancing auctions because the values required for various balancing auctions aren't as well defined as some other parts of the bidding system. Accuracy in balancing has always been notoriously weak, even among expert partnerships.

All pass to four spades and you wait for dummy with fear and trembling. The club Ace is led, and this is what you see:

♠ J952
♡ K1072
◇ AJ
♣ J52
□
♠ KQ1063
♡ AJ3
◇ Q8
♣ Q74

It seems that partner did credit you with a little more than you can actually produce. Maybe you should talk about this sequence after the session. Many players, incidentally, would have responded one *spade* with partner's hand. In case of more bidding, they could introduce their heart suit next, and play in either suit at the two level. Another example of planning ahead in the auction.

The contract has chances if they don't beat it immediately with a club ruff. But LHO switches to a low diamond at the second trick. You finesse, with no option, and the Jack wins the trick. You lead a trump to the King and LHO's Ace, and now they cash the club King on your left and continue with a third club. Luckily for you, RHO has to follow to all three clubs, so you win the third round. You draw two more rounds of trumps, finding that LHO had Axx to start with; and you cash the diamond Ace, collecting small cards from the opponents. With the contract on the line, how do you play the hearts?

■   ■   ■

The best way to find an answer to the problem is to try to reconstruct the concealed hands. Let's see. LHO had three spades to the Ace, and three or four clubs to the Ace-King. If he had six or seven black cards, he had six or seven red cards. Right? Now, how do you think his red cards would be divided? They must be divided pretty evenly—if LHO had as many as *five* hearts or diamonds, he would have opened the bidding with one of those suits. So his red suits should be divided 3-3, 4-2, or 4-3. The point is that LHO should have pretty even distribution all the way around. Now, what about high-card points? He had the spade Ace, diamond King, club Ace-King. That's fourteen. Suppose LHO had the heart Queen. He would have a balanced hand with sixteen high-card points. What would he have opened? Not one club. The heart Queen should be on your *right*.

To repeat, many people think that placing cards is strictly the province of the expert. But when placing the Queen of hearts on this hand is based on something so simple as counting to sixteen, there's no reason why *anybody* couldn't guess where the lady was hiding. In principle, it's a very simple process.

40

The Grand National Teams is an event that begins with eliminations at the grassroots level, and proceeds by stages to the Finals at the Summer National tournament. In a way, the pressure is worst at the local level, where a team with title aspirations knows that it should win easily, barring unforeseen "accidents." There is a lot to lose if things go badly, and little gratification for winning.

Playing in the GNT Qualifying, you sit down against one of the toughest pairs in the room—for you anyway: your wife and her mother! The little green men who arrange the draw are really in a mischievous mood today. If you lose this match, you'll never hear the end of it. And what if something bad happens, like a hesitation? If you call the Director over and protest, your wife may do something drastic, like withhold any further loaves of her delicious banana nut bread. The pressure is definitely on.

On the first board of the match, you pick up, as dealer:

♠ AJ4
♡ K10753
♢ 104
♣ AJ6

You open ONE HEART, and your mother-in-law overcalls ONE SPADE. TWO DIAMONDS from partner, pass on your right. It used to be that a two notrump rebid here promised extra values, but there were problems with that style. Opener sometimes had to rebid a less than robust major suit, or raise partner with three-card support and no extra values, instead of suggesting notrump as he dearly wanted to do. Nowadays, with many players willing to open one notrump with *any* balanced hand of medium strength, the two notrump rebid is better played to show a balanced *minimum.*

Partner raises your TWO NOTRUMP rebid to THREE NOTRUMP. All pass, and the opening lead is the spade seven. You see:

♠ Q62
♥ A4
♦ KJ983
♣ Q105
□
♠ AJ4
♥ K10753
♦ 104
♣ AJ6

How do you plan to make this hand?

■　　■　　■

The obvious should be considered first. Say you win the spade in hand and ride the ten of diamonds. RHO wins the Queen (you often *assume the worst* when planning your play) and returns a spade. LHO's suit is established, with the diamond Ace as a possible entry. Down one. Can you improve on that gloomy script? Clearly, you don't want to lose an early trick to RHO and then see a spade return. How about a diamond to dummy's *King* at trick two, playing LHO for Ax? Still no guarantees. Your mother-in-law has been known to overcall on anything, including a whim, and might not have the Ace of diamonds. And diamonds could be 3-3 anyway. Is there any point is postponing your attack on the diamond suit? Not much. Unless you want to rely on a 3-3 heart break plus a winning club finesse, you are going to need at least one diamond trick to get home.

The best play here isn't so hard after you spot it, but it might well be overlooked by a beginner, who is taught to lead *toward* his intermediate cards in taking finesses. You win the first trick with dummy's spade Queen and lead a low diamond *from the table.* Your object is to lose any early diamond trick to LHO, who cannot continue spades. If RHO jumps up with the Ace(!) of diamonds to return a spade, the diamond suit may well produce four tricks. And if RHO holds Qx(x)(x) of diamonds, she will need second sight to put the diamond Queen up in second seat, even though it would be the only way to defeat the contract.

If you can shut the spades out, you will almost surely have time to develop the tricks you need to make three notrump. Against best defense (they win the diamond Queen on your left, return a diamond to RHO's Ace, and a spade comes back), you may have to cash all your red-suit winners and throw LHO in with your last spade for a club endplay. Best of all, you might get to ask you wife why she didn't go right up with the Queen of diamonds in second seat.

One more thing. The spade Queen will win the first trick if you put it up. Apply the *Rule of Eleven.* RHO has only one spade higher than the seven, and it cannot be the King, since LHO would lead the spade ten from 10987x.

41

In all the World Championships and in many of the ACBL's most important events, the crucial matches are shown to an audience on *Vu-Graph* or *Bridgerama.* These are marvelous shows. The Vu-Graph is basically an overhead projector. Each hand in the match to be featured is written onto a transparency so it can be projected onto a screen for the crowd to see. The result from one table in the match is made known. Then the audience hears the bidding and play from the other table as it actually occurs, thanks to a telephone hookup to the playing room. As each trick is played to, the appropriate cards are marked out. The Bridgerama is a more elaborate setup, with lighted panels which blink out as the cards they represent are played.

If you've never been to one of these things, you've missed one good time. There is always a battery of expert analysts present, who try to predict what the players will do, and speculate on the final results of the deal. The audience, meanwhile, lives and dies with each mistake or brilliancy, and the suspense of waiting for a player to make what everybody can clearly see is the winning bid or play is enough to keep you on the edge of your seat. Good plays always bring a chorus of cheers from the audience, while a bonehead mistake is roundly booed. Of course, the players can hear nothing of this, which is just as well. It's all great fun.

You are on the U.S. Olympiad Team, and your match today has been chosen to be featured on Bridgerama. One slip, therefore, and the whole world will know about it. Scary, isn't it? This is your first chance to play to the gallery:

♠ AK742
♡ Q73
◇ A82
♣ J3

You are vulnerable, they are not. RHO deals and passes, and you open ONE SPADE. TWO CLUBS from partner. RHO now enters with TWO DIAMONDS. You have a sound minimum, so you decide to bid TWO NOTRUMP freely instead of passing around to partner. Partner now takes you back to THREE SPADES. What should you do next?

■   ■   ■

Back in the days when a two notrump rebid after a two-over-one response showed considerable extra values, and a major-suit opening was frequently made on four cards, partner's three spade preference would have been considered 100 percent forcing. Nowadays, it probably should not be forcing, just invitational. But partner probably thinks it's forcing, especially after you bid two notrump directly. So you had better not pass. As far as which game you should bid, spades seems preferable because you do not have the running tricks you would like to have for notrump. You will need time to develop some tricks, and that can be best done if you have a trump suit with which to control things. Also, you have the *primary* diamond value, which will be better for spades. If your hand were something like:

♠ AKxxx
♡ Jxx
◇ Q10x
♣ Ax

notrump would be more attractive. There would be a better chance you
could shut out the diamond suit and a better chance that, with your improved help for partner's clubs, you could run off some tricks in his suit.
(Maybe you shouldn't have even bid *two* notrump!)

Against FOUR SPADES, LHO leads the diamond Jack. Noting that
he is glad you didn't pass, partner tables:

♠ 853
♡ A62
◊ Q5
♣ AK742
□
♠ AK742
♡ Q73
◊ A82
♣ J3

Partner may have a chance to reconsider. The contract looks like uphill
work. Your chances are slim if trumps are 4-1 (unless, perhaps, clubs are
3-3). Given a decent trump split, you can make it if the heart King is
right, or if you can set up a club trick or two. RHO rates to have the heart
King for his overcall, but opponents sometimes do not have what they
should, so you had better plan to rely on clubs. To set up that suit against
a (likely) 4-2 break, you will need three entries to the table, two to ruff
clubs, one to cash the winner you establish. The three entries are there all
right; one in clubs, the heart Ace, and a diamond ruff. Just a little care and
timing is required of you. Don't forget, the Bridgerama audience is hanging
on every card.

■   ■   ■

To start, you *duck* the opening lead in both hands. If you win the
Ace and return a diamond right away, RHO could win and play a third diamond, forcing you to use of your entries too early, or more likely, allowing his partner to overruff the dummy. If you cover with the diamond
Queen and duck RHO's King, you might run into a diamond ruff, or a
heart switch that could knock out dummy's heart entry prematurely.

After winning the first trick, LHO continues a diamond to the
Queen, King, and Ace. You cash the high trumps, hoping for an even split,
and both opponents oblige by following suit. Now you play the Ace, King,

and another club, ruffing. RHO shows out on the third club, pitching a heart. You now use your *heart* entry to dummy in order to ruff a fourth club, establishing the fifth one. (If you were to use your diamond ruff as an entry at this point, RHO could discard another heart on the fourth round of clubs, and it might be his last one. He could then ruff your heart Ace when you tried to use it, and you would never see the fifth club you worked hard to set up.) RHO could have:

♠ QJx
♡ Jx
♢ K109xxx
♣ xx

After ruffing the fourth club, you ruff a diamond to dummy, and play the good club, pitching one of your little hearts. You must take ten tricks. If the good club is ruffed, your last trump will be a winner. Otherwise, the club is the tenth trick.

Just a little good technique, but the Bridgerama audience will surely give you at least a standing ovation.

42

There are a lot of people who would rather watch than play. And there are certain undeniable advantages the kibitzer enjoys. He can sit through an entire session and not make a single error, which is much easier on the ego; there are no pressures to cope with; and, provided all the players have a thick enough skin, he can second guess them, not to mention heckle, to his heart's content. There are, in fact, some kibitzers so obstreperous that a club might have to impose some rules on them to keep them in line. For example, there might be a rule that any kibitzer who offers a faulty analysis is obliged to buy a round of drinks for the table, or even pay off, based on the table stakes, what he would have lost by his error had he actually been in the game. Such rules, however, are likely to dampen the typical kibitzer's enthusiasm only a little.

Not long ago, I played in a "one-table team game." This turned out to be a real kibitzer's paradise. Our kibitzer (we brought one along) was charged with supplying an imaginary result from the "other table." The result we had when we actually played the hand, we IMPed against this bogus result so that we could pretend that the game was really a team-of-four. (You might try this sometime if you have an extra player who is a good analyst, imaginative, and can somehow remain impartial.)

Early in the evening, we encountered this exercise: you have this hand, which fails to arouse any passions in you to begin with:

♠ Q1052
♡ A863
♢ Q9
♣ K73

Nobody is vulnerable. RHO deals and passes, you pass and LHO opens ONE CLUB. Partner overcalls ONE DIAMOND, passed to you. What action do you take?

■   ■   ■

There are several possible actions. Two notrump, two clubs, and one notrump are all in the ballpark. You choose the last of these, disdaining the cue-bid because partner is less likely to have four cards in either major after his overcall (and because you wish, as always, to limit and describe your hand early). Over your ONE NOTRUMP, partner looks happy and leaps to THREE NOTRUMP. All pass.

The opening lead is the spade three, and this dummy hits:

♠ AK7
♡ J52
♢ AK8642
♣ 8
          □
♠ Q1052
♡ A863
♢ Q9
♣ K73

Some players would surely have doubled one club with partner's hand, but his plan was a good one. He wanted to get his six-card suit in to begin with. Then, if the bidding continued, say, two clubs on his left, pass, pass, he could double and describe his hand almost exactly. He could also double if it went one of a major, pass, one notrump, back to him. His jump to game is less easy to defend, though. He could have bid three diamonds or taken things a little slower with a two club cue-bid.

Meanwhile, how do you plan the play in three notrump? Hopefully, you know enough to think things over before touching a single card.

■   ■   ■

If diamonds split, you will make overtricks. The danger is that RHO might have Jxxx or 10xxx of diamonds (you can do nothing if he has J10xx). If he were able to win a diamond trick and come through your King of clubs, terrible things would happen. Your aim, then, will be to develop diamonds so that RHO can never win a trick in the suit, and the position is such that an avoidance play is available. You can lead a diamond from dummy and put in the nine from hand. If this loses to LHO, he can do nothing to hurt you, and the diamonds are now bound to run.

Suppose you let the opening lead run to your ten, go back to dummy with another spade, and make your diamond play. There is potential trouble with that approach. When LHO won the diamond, he could lead a third spade, killing dummy's last entry to the diamonds. Far better for you to win the first spade in dummy, disdaining the free finesse the opening lead tempts you with. The number of spade tricks you make here is negligible. You must set up the diamonds, and do it safely if you can, to make this game.

There must be ten thousand books on bridge that teach good technique. It is strange (to me) that there are so few texts that extol the potential rewards of total concentration at the table. Most of the mistakes that are made at bridge are just silly lapses, especially if the players in the game are experts, and possessed of good technique. On this deal, if you play low from dummy on the opening lead and then start thinking, it would be too late. The missing hands were:

♠ Jxxx   ♠ xx
♡ K10x   ♡ Qxx
♦ J   ♦ 10xxx
♣ AQJxx   ♣ 109xx

The declarer in our game, in case you're interested, played correctly, and scored up three notrump with an overtrick (he caught LHO in a spade-club position at the finish), and our kibitzer-adjudicator marked it down as a push! He was, he said, accustomed to watching—and imagining—only the best bridge.

43

More and more people seem to be making a living at bridge these days. There are the columnists, the cruise directors, the Tournament Directors, the bridge teachers. The most glamorous bridge-related occupation is probably that of the playing professional. There are a couple of hundred of these, well-known experts who hire themselves out as partners and teammates for ACBL events. Their fees are substantial, and it's definitely no Bohemian existence they live.

There are various reasons why somebody might hire a pro to play with. There are the egotists who want to be seen playing with someone known as a top expert. Then you have the altruists, who love to see the game played well, and are willing to pay for that pleasure. Of course, Master Points are the overriding consideration for many people. Personally, I have a mild aversion to playing with someone who just wants me to pimp a few Master Points that would be hard to come by otherwise. This kind of thing has always attached a strange stigma to the practice of playing professionally. But, luckily, not every client is like that. Many of them just want to *learn* some more about the game, and see playing with a professional bridge player as something like taking a playing lession from a golf pro.

Whatever your conception of what a bridge pro should be, your job is to give your clients what they have paid for. Playing in a Regional Swiss with a nice old lady who needs 7.85 Golds, you pick up an undistinguished hand:

♠ 853
♡ A1073
♢ AJ6
♣ J82

Only your side is vulnerable. LHO deals and passes, and partner quavers "A" CLUB. You'll have to try to ignore the implications of that. You respond ONE HEART, and LHO now comes in with ONE SPADE. Partner puts down her knitting, thinks for some time, and raises to TWO HEARTS. The long mull could mean anything. She could have raised you on a doubleton heart, trying to get you to be declarer! RHO passes. Should you bid again?

■　　■　　■

Not if partner may have questionable support, surely. But you *cannot* trade on any inferences available from partner's tempo, not if you are an ethical pro. Matter of fact, if you had a 50–50 guess about whether to go on here, an ethical player would feel bound to take the action that partner's huddle did *not* suggest. Luckily, you don't think that this particular decision is even close. You have 10 points, but your distribution is terrible. Just look at all the losers! Vulnerable games are nice, but here the chances of going down in three are greater than the chance of reaching game and making it. Besides, the tendency to bid every *vulnerable* game you can even sniff, at IMP scoring, doesn't apply so much to *short* matches. If you were playing a *one*-board match, and had to decide whether to bid a game, the vulnerability wouldn't matter at all. And it doesn't matter so much in a seven-board match either. It takes a lot of boards for the odds to bear fruit.

Two hearts is passed out. The opponents refuse to balance, which you suspect is probably a wise move on their part. They lead the spade King, and partner displays:

♠ A72
♡ KJ62
◇ K104
♣ Q93

□

♠ 853
♡ A1073
◇ AJ6
♣ J82

You were right about the "a" club opening, but the huddle before the two heart raise is a mystery. Maybe she was worried about a "free raise" with her minimum. This is a misconception that a lot of players have. A free *bid* is an action that strikes out for parts unknown, and so it may be declined with minimum values. But you can't afford to suppress a known fit, even if your hand is minimum. If you do, competition may shut you out of the bidding, so that you never get to show partner your support. So the term "free raise," even though it is often heard, is really meaningless.

Back to the play in two hearts. What is your plan?

■   ■   ■

You begin by ducking the first spade. This should be safe, since LHO neither opened with a weak two bid nor competed further. If he lacks the spade Jack, he may fear you have it and switch to something that may help you out. No luck, though. A spade is continued. You win the Ace, and *exit with a spade.* Your idea is to get the opponents to save you some guesswork in the other suits. LHO wins the third spade, as RHO follows suit. LHO overcalled on a four-bagger. At this point, any exit by LHO will help you. He finally gets out with a diamond, RHO puts up the Queen, and you win. Now, which opponent should you finesse for the missing Queen of hearts?

■   ■   ■

Neither one. Play the Ace and King of trumps. If the Queen falls, draw the last trump, cash your diamond winners, and go out looking for the club ten. If no heart Queen appears, however, you are almost as well off. Cash your diamond winners, and exit with a trump. The opponents are stuck again. They can either break the club suit, assuring you of a trick there; or give you a ruff and discard. Either way, you will make eight tricks.

At the other table, they climbed up to three hearts on your cards, and took lots of finesses in the play. Not all of them worked, and the contract went down a couple. The upshot was that you were that much closer to grinding out the 7.85 Golds. More important, your nice old lady watched the play at your table with interest, and you think it might have made an impression. Maybe she can help herself get the Gold the next time there is an *early throw-in* in the cards.

44

In most duplicate tournaments, two boards per round are played. Then you meet new opponents and two new boards. The main advantage in this scheme seems to be that if they nail you on the first board, you are given a chance to get a little revenge on the second one.

They just wrapped up four spades doubled against you on the opening board, so it's time for Nemesis to put in an appearance. Partner in particular looks determined to see that justice prevails. As dealer, you hold:

♠ AQ3
♡ K64
♢ AK963
♣ Q8

Too strong for one notrump opening with your eighteen-count *plus* a good five-card suit, you start with ONE DIAMOND. LHO overcalls ONE SPADE, and partner is in there with a *Negative* DOUBLE. (Negative doubles are a commonly played convention. Your partner's double, you have agreed, is not for penalties, but for *takeout*. He has one or both of the other two suits, but the wrong type of hand to bid one of them freely.)

You decide to leap all the way to THREE NOTRUMP, playing partner for at least seven points or so for his action (two notrump and a two spade cue-bid are other possibilities). Partner, after some consideration, puts it up to SIX NOTRUMP.

LHO leads a club, and this frightening dummy hits:

♠ 6
♡ AJ73
♢ J7542
♣ AJ3
□
♠ AQ3
♡ K64
♢ AK963
♣ Q8

Partner has lost his mind, of course. Even six diamonds might be a shaky proposition, since your spades could be headed by the King-Queen or King-Jack instead of the Ace. So six notrump is really hungry. Partner probably reasoned(?) that all the pairs holding your cards would bid a slam, so the ones in six notrump would get the top score. Since he is so short on high-card points, that is questionable logic. Not to mention that six notrump may well go down, which won't make his bid look good at all.

You duck the opening lead, and RHO wins the King. A spade comes back, of course, and you have to win the Ace. Plan the play from here.

■　　■　　■

Assuming there are five diamond tricks available, you still need the heart finesse, plus 3-3 hearts or a *squeeze*. You are about to cash the diamond Ace, when you see the chance for a little deceptive play. Crossing to dummy with a club, you lead the Jack of diamonds. If RHO plays low without thought, you plan to go up with an honor, hoping for the normal 2-1 break. But if RHO has the Q10x of diamonds, he will really have to be on the ball to duck smoothly. When you lead the diamond Jack, RHO is taken by surprise. He pauses, and is lost. Finally, he covers with the Queen, and LHO shows out as you win. You lead a heart to the Jack (displaying nerves of steel; you will go down a million if the jack loses, but that can't be helped—down one and down a million would be worth the same zero when your matchpoint score on this hand is figured). Then you cash the good club, and play a diamond to your nine. On the run of your diamond winners, LHO is squeezed. His hand is:

♠ KJ10xxx
♡ Q10xx
♢ —
♣ 10xx

When you play off the last diamond, he cannot keep both the King of spades and a guard to the heart suit. You will watch for the King of spades, and if it does not appear, you will assume that the hearts are ready to run.

For obvious reasons, this is called a "simple" squeeze. On second thought, I suppose it's not really so simple, since several conditions must be met before even a "simple" squeeze will function. But to execute this squeeze really is simple, because all you must do is cash *every one* of your winners. Don't hesitate to part with your last one, since the squeeze won't work otherwise.

You got up and staggered away from the table. Partner intercepted you as you headed for your next opponents. "Well," he informed you matter of factly, "we averaged the round."

45

Once I was playing in a Sectional tournament with a rather crochety old woman, long noted for her cantakerous ways at the bridge table. Partway through the game, she managed to get into an argument with one of our opponents. It didn't take much effort on her part. There was a difference of opinion about a bid somebody should or should not have made, I forget which. But pretty soon, spirits began to run high. Finally, after the recriminations had flown back and forth across the table for some time, my harassed opponent drew himself up and spouted, "Madam, I'll have you know that *I* am a Life Master." That may have been a miscalculation on his part. My not so fair lady promptly snapped, "Well, I've seen many a one who couldn't follow suit"!

Our table, or part of it anyway, broke up at this, and the opponents adjourned to the next table with one of them prominently sporting a hook in his gills. But you know, the irony is that there really are a great many Life Masters whose skills are suspect. The ACBL's player ranking system has a problem. Perseverence is as much a factor in achieving recognition as expertise at the game. In chess, I believe your rating can go up or down, depending on how well you fare against your peers. But at bridge, the Master Points just keep on accumulating. So, almost anybody can earn the highest playing rank the League has to bestow if he or she cares to spend enough time (and money). And no one seems really interested in changing things so as to better recognize true ability and dedication at bridge.

To my mind, the term "Master" has been a little misrepresented. Part of the charm of the game is that nobody ever really "masters" it. But I wouldn't consider somebody even close to being a "Master" unless he or she could eat up a hand like this one:

Playing in a Swiss Team match, with all the marbles on the table, you pick up:

♠ K4
♡ K63
◇ Q1053
♣ AKQ8

LHO opens ONE DIAMOND, passed around to you. Vulnerable against not, what should you do?

■   ■   ■

If the opponents were vulnerable, there would be a case for passing, settling for what could be a substantial penalty instead of a nonvulnerable game that you might not be able to bid even if you can make it. But at the current vulnerability, you decide to go out looking for a contract. If you were to miss a game, the loss would be damaging. To begin with you must DOUBLE. (A *balancing* one notrump here would show somewhat *less* than a normal one notrump opening.) LHO rebids TWO DIAMONDS, and partner comes in with TWO SPADES. You have a lot more than you might have had for a balancing takeout double, and partner should have a few values, so you figure you cannot bid less than THREE NOTRUMP.

All pass, LHO lays down a high diamond, and partner, commenting that he has a terrible hand, puts down:

♠ QJ96
♡ Q72
◇ J4
♣ J753

□

♠ K4
♡ K63
◇ Q1053
♣ AKQ8

LHO continues with a second high diamond at trick two, with RHO discarding a heart, and you win the third diamond, as a spade comes down on your right. How do you play from here?

■   ■   ■

This hand requires a delicate piece of timing. At trick three you must lead your *little* spade toward the dummy. LHO must duck, else you make three spade tricks and your contract. When dummy's Queen of spades wins, return to your hand with a club and lead a low heart. Again, LHO must duck his Ace, or you have nine tricks. After winning a heart trick with dummy's Queen, you will switch back to spades, and establish another trick there, for nine in all. If LHO is allowed to win one of your major-suit honors prematurely, he will establish his diamonds (with an Ace remaining as an entry) before you get nine tricks set up. Any other line of play would fail, as LHO's hand is:

♠ Ax
♡ AJx
◇ AKxxxx
♣ xx

Partner's hand did contain a lot of Queens and Jacks, but those cards are most useful at notrump, and they did produce some tricks with *your* high cards supporting them.

If you were to play this hand correctly and make it, I wouldn't care how many Master Points you had. You'd be a Life Master in my book.

46

The Swiss Teams event is responsible for a substantial rise in tournament attendance, and is much beloved by the players, especially the ones who walk away with a handful of fractional Master Points whether they play well or badly. But the Swiss can be a cruel and heartless event as well, at least for the expert players, who often find themselves in contention for the whole ball of wax. In a large field, the loss of just one match by 3 IMPs can send you plummeting from first place down to ignominy. In theory, you might put up two of the best sessions of your whole life to get into position to win, fifty-five flawless boards. And then one three-IMP error can make all your good bids and plays meaningless.

In more and more places, the Swiss is being scored by *Victory Points*. A certain number of VPs are available in each match. A win by a large margin gets you most or all of the Victory Points, and you still receive some if you lose a close match. This scheme, in which the team that earns the most VPs over the course of the whole event is the winner, is obviously more equitable than the fierce win-loss scoring. But Victory Points have a few flaws of their own, unfortunately. The boards for each match cannot be duplicated across the entire field; this means that sometimes you might have the misfortune to play a match in which a large margin of victory is impossible, because of several flat boards. And there is more work for the Directorial staff when the VP totals of all the teams must be kept up with. Nevertheless, I'd love to play in a Swiss with Victory Point scoring every time.

Playing in a Swiss (with win-loss scoring, so you'd best win at least three more IMPs than they do), you hold:

♠ K1064
♡ 4
♢ Q105
♣ KQ1075

You are "white against red" (you are not vulnerable, they are), and partner opens ONE DIAMOND. What is your response?

■   ■   ■

There are obvious problems. If you respond two clubs, and partner rebids two diamonds or two notrump, you cannot show your spades without failing to limit your hand and suggesting more strength. There will be rebid problems if you respond one spade, but at least you will get your major suit into the auction; so you try a ONE SPADE response. Partner's next bid is . . . TWO NOTRUMP. You still have no idea where you want to play, so you temporize again, with THREE CLUBS. If partner takes the opportunity to bid his diamond suit again, then six diamonds will probably have good chances. If he says three hearts, suggesting values in that suit, you can bid three notrump. If he tries three notrump himself, it will probably be all right. If he takes a spade preference, you will have to keep guessing.

But partner doublecrosses you and jumps to *FOUR* SPADES. That was liable to happen. He thinks you have longer spades than clubs, as your bidding does in fact suggest. He wanted to show you three really good spades by jumping. Maybe you should have responded two clubs after all. And what should you do over four spades?

■　　■　　■

It looks like partner would need just the right hand to produce six clubs or six diamonds, and since specific optimism in the bidding seldom pays off (partner *never* has exactly the right cards, in my experience; Barry Crane, the ACBL's top Master Point holder, has a suggestion for all his partners that I commend to you—"Never play me for certain cards, because I won't have them"), you decide to shoot it out in four spades. You probably belong in three notrump if six of a minor is no good, but that can't be helped now. The heart King is led, and you see that you should have been an optimist:

♠ AQ3
♡ J752
◇ AK84
♣ AJ
　□
♠ K1064
♡ 4
◇ Q105
♣ KQ1075

With partner holding that Jack of clubs and little waste in hearts, six clubs looks like a heavy favorite, while your four spades could get set. Not a good way to win a seven-board Swiss match. The heart King wins, and a low one is led next. RHO plays the ten. How do you play your way out of this?

■　　■　　■

We have seen that there are several ways to approach the play of a 4-3 fit. Scrambling tricks on a crossruff is impractical here, because most of your tricks are in the side suits and you want to draw trumps if possible. Various ways of keeping control are worth considering. The best way here is to eliminate the danger of the opponents' best suit by "drawing hearts." So, ruff the second heart, club to dummy, heart ruff, diamond to dummy, heart ruff. If you get overruffed at any time, you will probably be OK, with one of the outstanding trumps gone and dummy still in possession of three good ones. Next, cash your spade King, cross to dummy, and take the other two high trumps. If spades are 3-3, fine. If they are 4-2, start running your minor-suit winners. When the hand with the good trump ruffs in, he or she may be out of hearts and will have to lead something to you. (In fact, everybody may be out of hearts by now, since you led them four times.) Barring a very unfortunate lie of the cards, you will make at least four, and maybe five or six. And if you're really lucky, the contract at the other table will be three notrump, down on a heart lead, or six of a minor, off a heart trick and a trick in the wash.

47

There seem to be two fairly vociferous schools of thought on what constitutes an overcall. One school thinks of an overcall as competitive, lead directing, or obstructive in nature, and is willing to climb into the opponents' auction with any old hand that offers hope of achieving one of those goals.

Me, I like to play *sound* overcalls. To my mind, an overcall should be a constructive, well defined move, much like an opening bid. Once in a while, I miss out on a distributional game or a good sacrifice, but (1) I avoid heavy penalties; (2) I do not give away information about my hand when I am unlikely to be declarer; (3) I do not give away information that will help the opponents judge the auction; and best of all, (4) my constructive auctions after a sound overcall are much more precise and my side can judge its defensive prospects against any opposing contract as well.

I've never been enamored with the theory that the opponents, especially in this day and age of negative doubles, are always going to bid less accurately just because I overcall their one club opening with one spade on guts and not much else. If my suit is so good that I am certain I just have to have that *lead*, I may be able to make a weak *jump*-overcall.

Everybody knows that the "right" style in overcalling is whatever works best for you and suits your temperament at the table. I'm just telling you what has worked very well for me ever since I started to play tournament bridge.

You sit down to play in the Charity Game, and today you have just a slight extra stake in the proceedings. Your partner today is Melvin. You and Melvin have carried on a running battle over bidding styles for quite a while. You like to overcall sound, usually thirteen points or more. Melvin likes to get in there on any thirteen *cards* or more. But for once, Melvin has agreed to play "your way." Only trouble is, if things don't go well, you'll never hear the end of it. This is the first hand of the fateful session. Neither side is vulnerable, RHO opens ONE CLUB in front of you, and you hold:

♠ 74
♡ AKJ63
◇ AQ95
♣ Q7

You overcall ONE HEART, trying hard to suppress a smile, and you hear LHO pass and Melvin grit his teeth and raise to TWO HEARTS. You try THREE HEARTS, and Melvin gives you a grin that looks a little fiendish and bids FOUR HEARTS. All pass.

The club Jack is led, and you see:

♠ AQ853
♡ Q84
◇ 873
♣ 92
□
♠ 74
♡ AKJ63
◇ AQ95
♣ Q7

Game is no bargain, and worse, you can't blame the questionable contract on Melvin, who certainly has the values to accept one of *your* game tries. Perhaps you should have passed two hearts, devaluing your Queen of clubs; or tried for game with three diamonds, over which partner might have refused to bid game because of his terrible diamond holding. In the meantime, how do you play four hearts to salvage your pride? RHO cashes two club tricks and shifts to a diamond.

■   ■   ■

It was the mountaineer Mallory who, when asked why he wished to scale a peak, replied enigmatically, "Because it's there." The same sentiments should not be applied to taking finesses, however. When you take a finesse, you are making the assumption that it will work. If your assumption is unjustified, there is no point in taking any finesse.

Your Queen of diamonds wins the third trick. This is a finesse you expected to work. Now, as to the spades, you should not take any finesses. The spade King rates to be offside on the bidding. Your best play is to duck the first round of spades completely. Win the diamond return and play to the spade Ace. If the King falls on your right, you can ruff a spade to establish the suit, draw trumps ending (hopefully) in dummy, and take two diamond discards on the spades. If the spade King remains unplayed after two rounds of the suit, you will just have to hope for 3-3 spades, as well as 3-2 trumps. But the recommended line of play will gain over a futile finesse of the Queen of spades when RHO has the spade King doubleton.

48

When the dummy hits the table, the better declarer will plan as much of his play as possible before touching a single card. He will count his sure winners and/or his potential losers; decide at what point, if at all, to draw trumps; consider whatever problems there may be as to transportation, timing, and so forth. This type of planning is especially well known, and beginning dummy players must learn the importance of careful planning and avoid hasty play to be successful. There is another type of planning that is written up less often, and that is planning in the *auction*. On many occasions, it will not be enough for you to think only about what you should bid right away. You may have to look into the future, like a chess player, and arrange things in advance so that you will be comfortably placed to bid at your *next* turn. Or, you may need to make a bid designed to give your side an edge when the *play* starts.

Playing in a local IMP Team-of-Four league, with a round robin format, you pick up:

♠ AJ642
♡ 10
◊ 53
♣ AKQ84

With neither side vulnerable, your RHO deals and opens ONE HEART. Your call.

■   ■   ■

There is a good chance that the opposition is about to do a lot of bidding in the red suits. If you overcall one spade, any competition will oblige you to show your other suit at what may be an uncomfortable level. (For example, it could go two diamonds on your left, three diamonds on your right.) A two club overcall will leave you better placed to get both of your suits into the auction. *Don't* consider a takeout double with a hand like this—you need to start bidding your suits.

Sure enough, over your TWO CLUBS, LHO leaps to FOUR HEARTS. If this is passed back to you, you plan to bid four spades, and play game in whichever black suit partner prefers. But partner goes to FIVE CLUBS on his own, after some thought, and everyone passes.

A low heart is led, and dummy isn't entirely a welcome sight:

♠ Q73
♡ 6
◊ A962
♣ J10973
□
♠ AJ642
♡ 10
◊ 53
♣ AKQ84

So much for tactics. You'd be better off in four spades this time. Even so, the opponents might make five hearts if one of them has a black-suit void. To make five clubs, you will have to pick up the spades without loss. How would you plan the play?

■   ■   ■

You will have to find RHO with K, Kx, or 10985 in spades. Your objective in the play should be to learn as much about the distribution as possible, so that you can make the winning decision, if there is one.

RHO wins the heart Ace at trick one and shifts to a trump. You win and draw a second round, on which RHO shows out. Next, you must do a little spadework. Maybe, to be more accurate, a little "diamondwork." You lead a diamond toward dummy. LHO inserts the Jack, and you duck. A diamond is returned. You win the Ace and ruff a diamond. LHO plays low diamonds on the second and third rounds, and RHO plays the Queen and King. The ten is still out, and presumably LHO still has it. His second-hand play of the diamond Jack is strange enough, and would be impossible without the ten.

At this point, you know enough to make a decision about the spade suit. RHO is known to have started with one club and three diamonds. How many hearts do you think he has? Surely five or six. If RHO had a seven-card heart suit, he might have bid on to five hearts instead of selling out to five clubs. And LHO would have had a questionable leap to four hearts with only four-card support. So, RHO has at least three spades and maybe four. You have only one chance to bring the spade suit in. It's not much of a chance, but you have nothing to lose by trying it. You bang down the spade Ace. LHO flinches. The King appears on the table.

The IMP result on this board was no big deal. In fact, it turned out you lost a couple of IMPs when your teammates mysteriously sold out to four spades and somehow had eleven tricks made against them. (You never found out how the play went because they wouldn't talk about it.) But you gained in a more important way. The opponents were damaged psychologically by your miraculous play of dropping the stiff King of spades. They handled you with kid gloves from then on. They could have doubled you a couple of times and did not. And they stretched to compete instead of letting you get your hands on the dummy. You may have lost IMPs on this board, but this was the board that won the match for you.

49

Sometimes your side has all the cards and the opponents do not bid. Other times the opponents have all the cards and your side does not bid. (If you're like most bridge players, the second situation is more common than the first.) Then, there are the times when the bidding is competitive. *Both* sides have a fit of sorts and enough high cards to compete. In competitive auctions, there will inevitably be close judgment decisions to make. Should you sell out or take the push?

There is a good rule of thumb that can be applied to competitive decisions at the part-score level. Normally, you will *bid as high as the three level* if you have a fit and your share of the high-card strength. The times to make an exception are when you have bad trumps and there may be losers in your own suit; when you have values, particularly secondary values, in the opponents' suit; or when your distribution is unexciting. In such circumstances, you may do better to sell out to the opponents. To illustrate, say that partner opens ONE HEART, there is a TWO DIAMOND overall, you raise to TWO HEARTS, your LHO raises to THREE DIAMONDS, passed back around to you:

(a) ♠ xx (b) ♠ xxx
♡ Kxxx ♡ Jxx
◇ xxx ◇ Qxx
♣ KQxx ♣ KQxx

You would cheerfully bid three hearts with hand (a), applying the general rule of thumb. You have a decent hand, *four* trumps (important), and none of your values are especially good only for defense. On hand (b), you would pass and try to beat them. Your trumps are poor, the diamond Queen is wasted for offense, and your distribution is flat. It may be easier to make five tricks defending than nine declaring. (These examples are both clear cut. The close judgment decisions come on the in between hands.) Similarly, you would refuse to go to the *four* level in competition unless there was something out of the ordinary about your hand, some extra shape or support.

Fighting it out in the Trials to determine the U.S. International Team, you hold:

♠ KQ9752
♡ K62
◊ 863
♣ A

RHO opens ONE CLUB (they are playing a natural system) and you overcall ONE SPADE. TWO CLUBS to your left, pass, pass. With a six-card spade suit and fair values, you can afford to risk TWO SPADES. Pass, pass, THREE CLUBS. You pass this time, LHO passes, and partner goes to THREE SPADES. All pass.

The Queen of diamonds is led against you, and you see this dummy:

♠ J6
♡ A94
◊ K742
♣ 10532
    □
♠ KQ9752
♡ K62
◊ 863
♣ A

Partner used the general rule in competition. His Jx is adequate support for a suit you have bid twice, he knows that the high cards are fairly evenly divided, and most important, he has no values in clubs. If his holding in clubs had been Q9xx, he would have tried to beat three clubs rather than support your spades on a doubleton. As it is, he expects you to have a singleton club (and therefore, red-suit values), so that three spades may play well.

You duck the Queen of diamonds lead, and RHO plays the Ace! Not a bad start. A low club is returned, and you take your Ace. You lead a low spade to the Jack and Ace, and ruff the King of clubs return. Now, how should you continue? Is there any reason not to bang down the trumps from the top?

■   ■   ■

Before playing anything, try to reconstruct RHO's hand. If you could *reason* out his distribution, it would make things a lot easier, to say the least. RHO is known to have had the singleton Ace of diamonds and at most four clubs; LHO couldn't raise the one club opening to two without at least four-card support. But RHO can't have any fewer than four clubs either. With three clubs and one diamond, he would have had a five-card major suit somewhere, and would have opened in his major. RHO's distribution must have been 4-4-4-1. Easy! You go to the heart Ace and lead a spade to your nine, knowing that LHO will show out. After you draw the rest of the trumps, you can claim three, conceding another diamond and one heart.

Come to think of it, maybe *you* should modify the competitive rule a little. As well as you play the dummy, it might be right for you to bid one more where the average card pusher would sell out!

50

Playing with your wife in the Master Mixed Teams, one of the few tournament events still scored at Board-a-Match, you encounter a twofold problem. The first part of the problem is that the female half of your opposition is wearing a dress cut so low that you can see her kneecaps; this doesn't help your concentration much. (That's probably what it's designed to do.) Having applied your best strategy, which is to take one good long look and then forget it, you get back to playing bridge. The second part of your problem is this:

♠ A52
♡ AKJ863
♢ A93
♣ 2

You are vulnerable, they aren't. There are three passes around to you, and you start with ONE HEART. Will the opponents go quietly? Don't bet on it. TWO CLUBS on your left. TWO HEARTS from partner. THREE CLUBS on your right. There is a clear danger that they have a good save in five clubs, but you have little room for tactics here. You cannot risk trying to sneak up on them with three hearts (then four hearts, if you get another chance) because everybody may be out of bids. Partner certainly couldn't bid any more. And to bid a new suit will accomplish nothing constructive. You go ahead and bid FOUR HEARTS. Maybe they will think you are trying to stampede them into a phantom save, and let you play it. LHO and partner pass, but RHO with the dress is still there and huddles. Finally, it comes. "FIVE CLUBS." Should you go on?

■ ■ ■

Five hearts could be cold if partner has the right hand. But there was no certainty of even making four hearts, so a double could just as easily be right. Since you have no idea what to do, you PASS around to partner. Your pass is *forcing*, since the opponents have clearly taken a sacrifice against your game. Partner is invited to bid five hearts with a sound raise and no wasted values, but should double with a minimum raise or with a hand containing wasted club strength. A pass by you here says you are uncertain what course is best, but you are willing to hear partner bid five hearts. Similarly, a double would suggest that five hearts is questionable, and that, from your point of view, it is best to take what can be gotten from five clubs doubled. You do not promise to beat five clubs thirteen hundred, you just say you think a plus is more likely defending. Partner can still exercise his judgment.

Partner considers for quite some time, and comes out with FIVE HEARTS. All pass this, and the opening lead is the club Ace. You see:

♠ K7
♡ 10952
◇ KJ52
♣ 753
□
♠ A52
♡ AKJ863
◇ A93
♣ 2

Partner had a tough decision. The three small clubs (suggesting a singleton or void in your hand) and the *four*-card trump support argue for bidding. The lack of high-card strength says double. At least, if you go down in this, you can fuss at your spouse for guessing wrong. (Perhaps that's another cogent argument for the correctness of your forcing pass: "If someone is going to make the final error, let it be partner"!)

After winning the first trick, LHO continues with the club King, and you ruff. The contract really doesn't look too bad, but the opponents' bidding bodes ill. Sure enough, when you lay down a top heart, RHO shows out. Not unexpected, since the opponents would have gone for a likely 700 in their save if your side could have won a heart trick. Now you have to pick up the diamonds to make five hearts. You win another high heart, play a spade to the King, a spade to the Ace, and ruff a spade. LHO follows low, low, Queen. RHO follows with low spades the whole time. How should you play the diamond suit to take partner off the hook?

■ ■ ■

A finesse of the Jack cannot work. LHO is a passed hand, and so far, you have seen him play the Ace-King of clubs and the Queen of spades. He also has the heart Queen, so the diamond Queen must be on your right, else LHO would have opened the bidding. When a simple finesse can't be right, you may be able to fall back on a *backward* finesse. LHO had three hearts, at least three spades, and at least five clubs to overcall; therefore, two diamonds at most. If RHO has Q10xx(x), there is nothing you can do but go down one. But there is a chance otherwise. Play to the diamond King and lead the Jack. You may *pin* the ten on your left.

RHO's actual hand was:

♠ J10xxx
♡ —
◇ Qxxx
♣ QJ10x

If that hand had jumped straight to five clubs over two hearts, taking the sacrifice they would obviously have to take sooner or later *without delay*, you would have had a third problem. You could not afford to pass to partner over five clubs because you would not yet have shown him your extra strength. You would have to guess yourself what to do. And the "advance sacrifice" might cause you to guess wrong.

Meanwhile, if you made five hearts, take another long look at problem #1 as a reward.

51

"Standard American" is the bidding system most commonly used in the United States. It is basically what the old Goren style has evolved into over the past thirty years, with many gadgets, refinements, clarifications and improvements tacked on. In *Standard,* an opening bid of one notrump shows balanced pattern and sixteen-eighteen high-card points. Or maybe fifteen-seventeen, if you prefer. You can play whatever range you like, except that a more narrow range is desirable. A range like fourteen-nineteen will naturally make accuracy in the bidding more difficult.

When Edgar Kaplan and Alfred Shienwold constructed their own bidding system twenty-five years ago, they adopted a notrump range of *twelve-fourteen* HCP. The "weak" notrump was unleashed. The weak notrump has several theoretical advantages: A common type of hand is described in just one bid; it is preemptive; the opponents may be afraid to enter the auction and may have trouble finding their best spot if they do come in; responder, knowing his partner's approximate strength and pattern, is well placed to compete or make penalty doubles.

On the negative side, there is the chance of a substantial penalty if the opponents are able to double one notrump. And constructive bidding can sometimes be hampered; you might open one notrump and play right there when an eight- or nine-card fit was available in some suit.

Perhaps the most striking thing about the weak notrump is that the players who do use it tend to defend its efficacy with passionate vigor.

Playing K-S is a one session matchpoint game, you pick up:

♠ AJ4
♡ 108
◇ AJ953
♣ K74

You open ONE NOTRUMP and partner raises to THREE NOTRUMP, ending a brief auction. (Another advantage of the weak notrump is seen here; such prosaic auctions as this give away little information and make the defense of your game that much harder.) LHO leads the King of spades, and this dummy comes down:

♠ 852
♡ AJ5
◊ Q8642
♣ AJ

□

♠ AJ4
♡ 108
◊ AJ953
♣ K74

RHO plays the spade six on the first trick, and you decide to duck. LHO thinks it over and shifts to the heart Queen, which you win. You attack diamonds by leading the Queen. Perhaps this will induce a cover from Kx, but it is really the correct technical way to play the suit anyhow. You intend to finesse for the King here (the percentage play), and leading the Queen to begin with will save you a trick if RHO has all three of the missing diamonds.

Your diamond finesse loses to LHO. A heart goes to RHO's King, and a spade comes quickly back. You win this trick, and must now decide whether to take your nine tricks and run, or risk the club finesse for an overtrick. This would be no problem at IMPs or rubber bridge, where making sure of what you've bid is the important thing. But it's a definite headache at Pairs. What is your inclination?

■ ■ ■

Drawing inferences from the opponents' play and acting on them is a critical part of expert declarer play, especially in a Pairs event, where you need big scores to win and must leave no stone unturned to get them. It is right to take the club finesse here. Think about it. Would LHO shift to the *Queen of hearts* at trick two with nothing in clubs? Surely not. He'd lead a club over to whatever hypothetical strength his partner might hold in clubs. Wouldn't you?

You lead a club to the Jack, and it holds. So you make four, for what should be a fine score. Even if the club finesse had inexplicably lost, you would have still made three if RHO was out of spades. The weak notrumpers, I'll bet, would probably give most of the credit for this result to the bidding.

52

Anytime there is a bridge tournament, the local players seem to capture more than their rightful share of the honors. (I just returned from a National tournament, with most of the country's best in attendance, and two hometown ladies won the Life Master Womens' Pairs, a major championship.) Perhaps the fact that the locals get to sleep in their own beds and have to cope with rather less disruption in their daily routine has something to do with it. But there is also the incentive factor to consider. Playing in front of the hometown fans, you just naturally want to put up a strong showing. And so you try that much harder, and sometimes your results can show it.

Playing in the Masters' Pairs at your very own Sectional, with your local reputation squarely on the line, you hold:

♠ Q10632
♡ K4
◊ AJ74
♣ Q2

Neither side is vulnerable and RHO deals and passes. What is your action?

■ ■ ■

I might pass this hand in first seat, with the bad suit and the lack of prime values, but I'd be scared to pass in *second* seat at matchpoints. Partner might be under some pressure in fourth seat if he has a very borderline opening with no great length in spades, and the hand might get thrown in when we could make a partial, or even a game. With a decent hand in second seat, and especially with some length in the boss suit, you get things going with ONE SPADE. LHO passes and partner responds THREE SPADES, forcing as you are playing. No choice, you must go on to FOUR SPADES.

The club three is led and partner appears to be a little light as well:

♠ KJ95
♡ A85
◇ K103
♣ J95

□

♠ Q10632
♡ K4
◇ AJ74
♣ Q2

Partner would have opened this time after three passes, but he would have tapped the table quickly over any spade response you made, and your side would have missed this game, which you surely need to bid and make to score well at matchpoints.

RHO wins the club Ace, and returns the club four to LHO's King. A third club is won by dummy's Jack. You play a spade to your Queen and LHO's Ace, and win the spade return, noting that trumps have split evenly. Everything seems to depend on the diamond guess, but you can postpone that for just a minute. First, you play three rounds of hearts, ruffing the last one. LHO follows: low, nine, Jack; and RHO follows with low hearts all the way. Now, how would you attack the diamonds?

■ ■ ■

LHO is known to have started with four clubs, judging from the opening lead, and two spades. He had at least J9x of hearts. Could he have more hearts? Perhaps QJ9x, or J109x, or QJ109x? Unlikely. In that case, the opening lead would have been a heart, away from his sequence, not a dangerous club away from his King. Barring any very subtle false cards, LHO had three hearts only. So, he must have had four diamonds, and RHO only two. In that case, the odds are four to two that LHO had any particular diamond, including the Queen. So you should be inclined to take your make-or-break finesse through him.

If it works, who knows? Maybe the local partisans will carry you around the table on their shoulders.

53

Playing in the Reisinger Teams, a prestigious National Championship scored at Board-a-match, you encounter a pair who have not only an overflowing Convention Card, but also a sheaf of typewritten pages lying on the table. Their bidding system and agreements, they inform you, just won't fit onto one tiny Convention Card.

There are quite a few excellent books out that list and discuss just about all the conventions that are commonly played in tournament bridge. The books have gotten very thick lately. Your options if you want to play lots of gadgets are almost unlimited. And, to be sure, there are many pairs who fervently believe that if they employ enough of the right conventions, their bidding ills will disappear.

Even though plenty of science is all well and good, superior bridge players will beat you no matter what methods they are using in the auction. It really matters less what conventions you play than that you and partner have a thorough understanding of the ones you *do* play. A firm knowledge of your bidding system as well as your favorite partner's *style* in the bidding will pay dividends. The very best partnerships have discussed their bidding methods for hours upon hours, not even counting the time they spend on artificial gadgets. So there might be a few rough edges *your* partnership could afford to polish up.

If you do want to add a new convention to your arsenal, consider carefully. Any worthwhile convention should be simple to use and effectively do the job it was designed for; it should not cost you a natural bid that might be more useful to have available; and the chance to use it should come up often enough that you are willing to invest the mental energy to remember it. There is no point in appending a convention that you never have occasion to use.*

On the first board of the round, Science is vindicated as your opponents have an artificial, complex-sounding auction to reach a slam that is laydown. Then you pick up:

---

*Hugh Kelsey's analogy comes to mind. He mentions a golfer, worn out from carrying too many clubs in his bag.

♠ 5
♡ QJ109752
◇ —
♣ AQ1063

LHO is dealer and passes, and partner opens ONE NOTRUMP. For no very good reason, you choose to blast into SIX HEARTS. Partner could have the perfect hand that will make seven cold, or he might have (gruesome thought) three small hearts, and you will fail embarrassingly in six. The only advantage in leaping straightaway to slam is that you are probably going to bid six anyway, and a prosaic auction will give the opponents no help on defense. Partner could have a hand like:

♠ KQxx
♡ Kxx
◇ AJx
♣ Kxx

and now they have to cash out to beat you. Actually, you do have an ulterior motive for your majestic shot in the dark. You want to provide a startling contrast to the first hand.

All pass to your six hearts, the opponents not without some snickers, the spade King is led, and the dummy is suitable:

♠ A92
♡ A63
◇ KQ63
♣ K72
□
♠ 5
♡ QJ109752
◇ —
♣ AQ1063

You take the spade Ace and huddle. They will surely reach this slam at the other table, so whether you make six or seven can be critical. The percentage play in trumps with ten cards missing the King is to finesse. Can you see any way to improve your chances here?

■ ■ ■

Suppose you dig for a little pertinent information. Lead the *King of diamonds* from dummy at the second trick. If RHO has the Ace, he will have to be a genius not to cover; so if the Ace does not appear, you can safely assume that LHO has it. LHO also has the King and Queen of spades, from the opening lead, so if he has the diamond Ace, the heart King should be offside. If LHO had it, he would have opened the bidding. (There are three missing Jacks, and LHO probably has at least one of them.)

The strategy of trying to smoke out the location of the diamond Ace is called a "discovery" play. If you are able to place the heart King in RHO's hand, you will play for the drop instead of taking a routine finesse.

No matter what happens, don't you and partner forget to compliment each other on your careful auction.

54

In a typical American Pairs' tournament, the boards are passed from table to table so that most or all of them are in play somewhere on every round of the game. The players do not know what their matchpoint score on each board will be until the game is over and all the results are in (unless they have become highly skilled in *estimating* their score as they go along). However, in some tournaments, mostly in Europe and in some of the World Bridge Federation events, there is "Barometer" scoring. The *same* boards are in play at *every* table during each round, so that the results can be computed and made known immediately. Every pair in the field knows its standing from the beginning of the session to the end. The logistics of running such a tournament are formidable, but it certainly makes for greater enjoyment for the players.

Playing in a tournament with Barometer scoring, you come to the last round of the event in mild contention for the lead. Therefore, you know you need to finish with two excellent results to have a chance at winning. The first board gives you a score only slightly above average, so desperate measures are in order on the second one. Your hand is:

♠ AK6
♡ A109642
◊ K4
♣ 73

Partner opens ONE DIAMOND, you respond ONE HEART. He rebids
TWO CLUBS. You resist an impulse to jump to three notrump in favor
of a temporizing TWO SPADES. Your hand has too much slam potential
(all top cards!), especially when partner's strength is not yet known. The
two club rebid could conceal a seventeen- or eighteen-point hand. Partner's next bid is THREE DIAMONDS, and things begin to look up. His
auction suggests six or seven diamonds and four clubs, *with extra strength.*
With a doggy 6-4, he would just rebid two diamonds at his second turn,
and limit his hand to a minimum right away. His actual sequence says
that he would have accepted a game try if you had issued one at *your*
second turn, so he has at least a little extra, fifteen high-card points or
more. Your top cards will cover whatever losers partner has in the majors,
so you decide you might as well Blackwood into slam.

Partner shows two Aces over your FOUR NOTRUMP, so you continue with FIVE NOTRUMP, and he shows one King. (Most players
agree that five notrump here suggests interest in a grand slam, and partner
is allowed to jump to seven by himself with certain hands; since you have
the King of his long suit, that won't happen here.) Now you have to decide which slam to bid. What is your choice?

■ ■ ■

You have already assumed that partner's diamonds are very good,
so eleven tricks can be counted. And partner should have another card
somewhere, or perhaps a seventh diamond. Since you need a particularly
good score at this stage, you try SIX NOTRUMP.

All pass, LHO leads a spade, and the dummy is about what you
hoped for:

♠ 93
♡ K
♦ AQJ1073
♣ AJ104
□
♠ AK6
♡ A109642
♦ K4
♣ 73

(While you are thinking about that hand, take a look at another one:

Dummy		*Declarer*
♠ Ax		♠ KQxxx
♡ xx		♡ Kx
♦ xxxx	□	♦ AKQ
♣ xxxxx		♣ AQx

Declarer is in three notrump and wins a heart lead with his King. The top diamonds reveal a 4–2 break there. How should declarer play? He can try for a 3–3 spade split, or cross to dummy with the spade Ace and take the club finesse. The finesse is a 50–50 proposition, while a 3–3 split will occur a little more than one third of the time. So the finesse is the better *percentage* play.)

You will often meet hands where there is nothing for you to do but determine the best line of play on a strictly mathematical basis. An elementary knowledge of percentages is useful for carrying out whatever simple calculations are possible right at the table. Back to the first hand. What do you think the best play is?

■ ■ ■

Win the spade lead and cash the heart King. If an honor drops, you will come back to the diamond King and set up a heart intermediate for your twelfth trick. Assuming nothing interesting happens on the first heart, you must decide whether to continue hearts or shift over to clubs and take a double finesse in that suit. The double finesse is 76 percent to bring in an extra trick. What are your chances in hearts? The odds on a 3–3 split are 35½ percent and added to that are the chances that somebody will hold the doubleton Jack or Queen. There will be a doubleton heart somewhere about 48 percent of the time and that doubleton will contain one of the missing honors in nine or fifteen cases. So the additional chance from that source comes to almost 29 percent. Your prospects from the heart suit are over 64 percent, not including the chance of a singleton honor. But that is still inferior to the club play.

55

Tournament bridge is a timed event. You are given a certain number of minutes to play two or three hands, and if you fall behind, the Tournament Directors will hover over your table, exhorting you to hurry and get caught up. Penalties are possible for chronic offenders, because excessive slow play by one table in a Pairs tournament affects other tables and can be unfair to the other players. In a social game, of course, there isn't any sort of formal time limit (but there are the complaints at the table, and the occasional player who is so slow that nobody will play with him).

Even in a tournament, I've never seen any really good player who minded if his opponent took a little extra time to think about a tough problem. We all face difficult decisions at the table, after all. One trouble with most people who are slow is that they are inclined to huddle when there is really nothing much in the way of constructive thinking to be done. There is a big difference in analyzing a problem situation with a clear train of thought, and sitting there waiting for some lightning bolt of inspiration to strike you. A fatuous huddle can only do your side harm. You (1) tell the opponents that you have no clear cut bid or play to make; (2) waste valuable mental energy that could be better used another time (don't let anybody ever tell you that *fatigue* isn't a factor in who wins at bridge); (3) put pressure on your partner to maintain his objectivity in the bidding and play; he's supposed to *ignore* your hesitation in choosing *his* next action, but that is sometimes easier said than done.

Say that the opponents have bid one notrump-three notrump. You have to make the opening lead from:

♠ A10x
♡ Qxx
◇ J10x
♣ xxxx

You could think about it for three years and not have any better idea
what the best lead was. So don't stew. Pick something out and put it on
the track. There are many similar situations that players face in a typical
session that do not lend themselves to any hair splitting analysis. It is dis-
courteous at best to spend any great amount of time on them.

Playing in a rubber game where all the players are slow, you pick
up:

♠ 4
♡ AJ983
◇ 752
♣ KQ42

Your partner opens ONE CLUB, with neither side vulnerable, and RHO
DOUBLES. What is your action?

■ ■ ■

Even though you have ten high-card points, this is not the time to
redouble. Sometimes, when you have an offensively oriented hand in this
situation, you cannot spend a round of bidding to redouble. You have to
start describing what you have right away. In this case, you want to show
a decent hand with good hearts, plus some club support. If you redouble,
it might go (say) one spade on your left, two spades on your right; and
now you wouldn't have room to show all the features of your hand
without risking a minus. So, you just bid ONE HEART for the time being,
planning to support clubs later. LHO passes and partner disappears into an
interminable mull. Finally, he emerges with TWO HEARTS. Great. You
know from partner's failure to raise promptly that he doesn't have a classic
two heart bid. But you are worth a shot at game over a raise, so being an
ethical player, you go on and bid FOUR HEARTS, even though the dummy may be a disappointment.

The spade Jack is led, and partner's hand is an enigma:

♠ A863
♡ KQ10
◇ 1063
♣ A63

□

♠ 4
♡ AJ983
◇ 752
♣ KQ42

What partner was thinking about all that time is anybody's guess. Did he think his support wasn't good enough to raise a suit you had mentioned in spite of the takeout double? Did he think you had psyched? Was he wondering where to take his wife for dinner? That must be it; because nobody could work up any real sweat wondering what devious action to take over one heart.

You seem to be in a good contract nevertheless. There are several possible lines of play. You could simply draw trumps and try to find the clubs splitting 3-3; that's about a 36 percent chance *a priori*, but probably less than that on this hand, after RHO's takeout double. An improvement on that line would be to draw only two rounds of trumps before trying clubs. You would still be safe if clubs were 3-3, and if somebody had one or two clubs *and* one or two trumps, you would be able to ruff your fourth club in the dummy safely. Can you find a line of play that is better still?

■ ■ ■

The very best percentage is available here by playing to *reverse the dummy*. Win the spade Ace and ruff a spade immediately. Go back to dummy with a trump and ruff another spade. Return to dummy with another trump. Now, if trumps have split 3-2, ruff a fourth spade, play a club to the Ace, draw the last trump, and cash your clubs. You might even make five. If trumps turn out to be 4-1, you will have to switch back to clubs while a trump remains in dummy; you may still make four. Clubs may split, or the hand with the long clubs may also have the long trumps. (If somebody ruffs one of your high clubs and returns their last trump, you will go down two instead of one, but you cannot ruff dummy's last spade before you play clubs—if RHO had three spades and three clubs in addition to four trumps, he would discard a club on this trick.)

By the way, couldn't you play a little faster?

56

The Stayman convention is perhaps the best known of all conventions, after Blackwood. But while Blackwood is surely the most abused convention, there being uncounted times when it is completely misapplied by players who don't know any better, the proper use of Stayman can involve close questions of judgement, and even experts would disagree in certain situations whether the use of Stayman would be appropriate.

Most everyone agrees that using Stayman is questionable when your major suit is very poor, or when your distribution is completely flat (remember, however, that *partner's* hand may contain a little shape), or when you have a great many secondary values (Queens and Jacks), so that you may have too many losers in a ten-trick game and only a nine-trick game will make. There is also one other time when you may forego Stayman, especially at IMP scoring or rubber bridge.

Playing in a Mens' Swiss Teams (a tough event), you pick up:

♠ KQ10
♡ K4
◇ A83
♣ K10963

Your one notrump opening is supposed to show sixteen–eighteen HCP, but you decide to treat your hand as a sixteen-pointer because of your good intermediates, your five-card suit, and your lack of Queens and Jacks. Partner raises your ONE NOTRUMP opening to THREE NOTRUMP, and all pass.

The Jack of hearts is the opening lead, and you see this dummy·

♠ 852
♡ AQ52
◇ Q4
♣ AJ52
□
♠ KQ10
♡ K4
◇ A83
♣ K10963

Partner undoubtedly chose to omit Stayman because he had so much high-card strength. He figured that three notrump would almost surely come home on sheer power, whereas a bad trump split might beat four hearts, even if there were a fit in hearts available. His decision would be less attractive at matchpoint scoring. If your side had a 4-4 heart fit, you might be able to score 450 or 480 in the suit game, while notrump would produce only 430 or 460. At IMPs, though, partner preferred what he thought would be the safest game.

Incidentally, how do you play three notrump for nine sure tricks? You don't want to have any slip-ups, right? Could anything go wrong?

■ ■ ■

If the clubs come in for five tricks, you will make a million. But if that suit only produces four tricks for you, you will need to set up one trick in spades to make your game. Assume, then, that clubs fail to break. Say that LHO has Qxx. He wins the third club and . . . shifts to a diamond. You might be in big trouble. If RHO turned up with KJxx of diamonds or K10xxx, and the spade Ace for an entry, the opponents would take five or six tricks before you manage nine.

You will be safe from a potentially damaging diamond play through the dummy if you just be careful to keep LHO out of the lead early. The correct play, therefore, is to cash the club King and lead a club to dummy's Jack. If this wins, super. If it doesn't, the opponents can't lead anything that will embarrass you, and you will have time to establish the spade trick you need.

The easiest looking hands are often the ones that deserve a little extra care. Think to yourself, "What circumstances could possibly keep me from making this?" When you see the answer, take appropriate precautions.

As for the bidding, the time you are anxious to play in a 4-4 fit, arrived at by way of the Stayman convention, is when you need a trump suit to keep control of the play, and, more important, when you *need* the *extra tricks* that the *trump suit* will provide to make game. If you have another good source of tricks, an abundance of high cards for instance, then playing in the major suit may be a needless risk.

57

Your opponent in a local tournament is a typical Machine Gun Kelly type who plays to every trick without apparent thought. You will meet many players like this. They intimidate you by slapping down their cards at a terrifying rate of speed, and it is easy to get caught up in the ferocity of their tempo. You don't want anybody to think that you can't play as fast as he or she can, so you play on impulse and wind up making a silly error. The fast player is most dangerous when he is declarer and can control the rate of play a little better. But no matter who is declarer, you just have to try and play at the pace you find comfortable and not let yourself be stampeded by anybody.

Both sides are vulnerable on the first board out, and your hand is:

♠ 5
♡ AKJ53
◇ J1062
♣ A83

RHO, the speed merchant, opens ONE SPADE (before you get your cards sorted, of course). It is dangerous for you to take any action here. It always is, when your RHO has opened and you know nothing about what your LHO may be lurking with. But it is just as dangerous to pass and risk being shut out, especially when you are short in the opening bidder's suit. Suppose you decide to get in there. Do you double or overcall?

■ ■ ■

If you double, you must pass if partner responds cheaply. You are by no means strong enough to double and then bid your hearts if he responds in a minor. So a double stands to miss a 5-3 heart fit, a potential disaster at matchpoints. At IMP scoring, you might decide to double because that is a more flexible action and gives you more chance of avoiding a big penalty. (It is true that a two heart overcall might work out better even at IMPs; if you have a *game*, it is probably in hearts; but finding the right part score could win you some IMPs as well.) Here, you finally settle on a TWO HEART overcall.

LHO raises to TWO SPADES, and partner looks worried and raises you to THREE HEARTS. You pass this, since your hand is minimum for a vulnerable, two level action, and you buy the contract.

LHO leads the spade Jack, and the dummy is upsetting:

♠ 9842
♡ Q6
♢ KQ73
♣ J72

□

♠ 5
♡ AKJ53
♢ J1062
♣ A83

Partner thought he had to compete, and it is true that you could have had rather more for your two heart bid. (You would often have a six-card suit.) Accuracy after a two level overcall is difficult, because there isn't much room for investigation below the level of game.

The tricks to make three hearts are there if you can find a way to take them. RHO quickly plays the spade seven on the first trick. LHO continues with the spade ten and RHO overtakes with the Queen. How should you plan the play? (Take your time. No points awarded for speed.)

■ ■ ■

This will be a snap if trumps are 3-3. But a 4-2 break is more likely, especially since the opponents look confident about their defensive prospects. Say you ruff the second spade, and play trumps. Against a 4-2 split, you will have to exhaust your trumps to draw all the outstanding ones, and then, if RHO has the diamond Ace, you will go down. Spades will be cashed against you. Suppose that LHO has the diamond Ace. If you ruff the second spade, draw (four rounds of) trumps, and lead a diamond, they will still beat you. LHO will win and lead his last spade for RHO to run the suit.

The best play should be getting clearer. You must discard a club on the second spade and ruff the *third* round. Then draw as many trumps as you have to, and lead a diamond. If the trumps are 4-2 and the diamond Ace is on your right, you will still go down, but you never could have made the contract in that event. If LHO has the Ace of diamonds, however, your holdup will have done its work. With no more spades to lead, he will have to let you back in with a minor suit to take the rest of your tricks.

The opposing hands were actually:

LHO		RHO
♠ J10x		♠ AKQxx
♡ xx		♡ xxxx
◇ Axx	□	◇ xx
♣ Qxxxx		♣ K10

This was the first board of the round, we said. And you took your time and made it. Even so, with MGK declaring the second hand, you still finished the round in plenty of time for a quick trip to the bar. There are certain other advantages to being a speed demon.

58

The tournament schedule had been heavy and you had played somewhere for six weekends in a row. So on the seventh weekend, you rested. You took a cruise to the Bahamas. Mostly, this was at the behest of your spouse, who complained bitterly that the only time you darkened the door of your house was to pick up fresh clothes for the next tournament. But there was bridge aboard the ship. Not that it was a full-fledged bridge cruise, with lectures, and duplicates twice a day. Just some easygoing rubber bridge games, for less-than-frightening stakes. By the second day out, you began to suffer withdrawal symptoms, and pretty soon, you were sneaking out of your cabin, away from the boredom of the sunbathing and shuffleboard, and up to the bridge game. At first, you were content only to watch, but finally, you thought it couldn't hurt to play a hand or two. So that's where you were when you were located. Playing bridge with three strangers.

On one of the early hands, you held these tickets:

♠ A4
♡ 752
♢ A8642
♣ K63

Both sides were vulnerable, and your partner, a severe looking middle-aged lady with a very sharp nose opened ONE CLUB. You responded ONE DIAMOND, resisting a strong impulse to bid some number of no-trump before partner could. Your lady looked over the rims of her glasses and bid an owlish ONE HEART. At this point, your options in an unfamiliar partnership were severely limited. In some of your regular partnerships, you could bid a nonforcing two notrump or three clubs, or even temporize with one spade(!). (The bid of the *fourth suit,* a forcing bid, is used by many partnerships as a convenient mark-time action that obliges partner to tell more about his hand.) With this partner, though, you just bid ONE NOTRUMP. She would think two notrump was forcing, and anyway, she is likely to find another bid over one notrump with anything more than a minimum. Sure enough, partner raised you to TWO NO-TRUMP, and you went on to THREE NOTRUMP. All passed. To your surprise, LHO led the club four. But you weren't surprised for long.

♠ K1083
♡ AKQ4
♢ K5
♣ 975
    □
♠ A4
♡ 752
♢ A8642
♣ K63

Another short club addict. It would have served her right if you had had two small clubs. There sure are a lot of casual players who think that if they just open one club, everything will somehow turn out just fine. They think that some sort of mystic significance is attached to a one club opening, that it asks partner not to pass, or to bid one diamond with a bust, or for a major suit, or for a weather report, or something. I've seen people open one club, for reasons best known to them, with two small clubs and five good spades. The poor old club suit, like Rodney Danger-field, just doesn't get no respect. And actions like partner's on this deal lead to absurd contracts about as often as they gain anything from the preparedness or the deceptive angle.

Trying to conceal your chagrin at the bidding (it could have been worse; you could have improvised with one spade at your second turn; you would have had a hard time wriggling out of *that* one), you win the first trick, capturing RHO's Queen. How should you plan the play from here?

■ ■ ■

You have eight top tricks, and the ninth could come from either a favorable diamond or heart split. But you can't try for a diamond split if the opposition can win their diamond trick and cash enough clubs to set you. If clubs are 5-2, you just have to hope that hearts are 3-3. Since everything seems to depend on the way clubs divide, you must return a club at the second trick and let the opponents take their club winners, if they will. If clubs turn out to be 5-2, the hearts will have to split for you (or a squeeze will have to develop; but your squeeze chances are dimin-ished because you will have to make some discards on the clubs and give up on some of those possibilities).

Suppose clubs are 4-3. After they cash three club tricks, you can win the return and *duck* a diamond. This play will allow you to see if the diamonds split without risking the loss of two fast tricks if they do *not* split. This way, you get to test *both* red suits, making your contract if you get a helpful break in either one.

As it turned out, the shipboard bridge game beckoned so often that you came home with *less* of a tan than you had to start the cruise. Your spouse got lots of sun and recreation, but you ended up needing a vacation to recover from your vacation. Your spouse, however, alleged that the next trip she took with you would be to a deserted island.

59

The *Laws of Duplicate Contract Bridge* includes a lengthy section called the "Proprieties." Here you will find the gospel on such nontechnical matters as ethics at bridge, hesitations, conduct at the table, and so forth. As you no doubt know, there is a strict code of ethics adhered to in tournament bridge. The stronger the players in the game, the higher the standard of ethics is likely to be. A true expert prizes his reputation as an ethical player above all else.

The Proprieties say that it is improper to draw inferences from partner's hesitations, mannerisms, vocal inflections, or anything of an extraneous nature that could give you an unfair edge. But this imposes a strain on human nature. Against some players (of less than expert caliber) you might run up against a little of what Edgar Kaplan once called "That Old Black Magic."

Suppose you are playing an established partnership, and their bidding is:

OPENER	RESPONDER
1 ♣	1 ♡
1 ♠	3 ♣

Is the three club bid forcing or not? Maybe the opponents have discussed this sequence (as you and your partner surely have), and they *know* whether or not it is forcing. But even if they haven't talked about it, there may be a sort of almost intangible *feeling* imparted by the three club bid that will suggest whether the bidder has a very good hand or just a fair one. Pairs that have played together over a long period of time often know each other so well that they have an edge in this and similar situations. If based on strength, the three club bid may be made promptly and with a tiny bit of unconscious emphasis. And opener will be aware of this, if only in his subconscious. That's the Old Black Magic. Could be that you think I'm a little paranoid about this, but believe me, this sort of thing can crop up in any partnership. Even the most actively ethical player can't make every single bid in the same even tone of voice.

The ACBL apparently recognizes that the problem exists, even among expert pairs, because it has begun to employ *screens* and *bidding boxes* in the late stages of some of its Championships. The screens are placed diagonally across the table, and prevent you from seeing your partner during the bidding and play. The bidding boxes are of European origin. Every bid from one club to seven no trump, as well as pass, double, redouble, Alert, Director, etc. are printed on color-coded cards that fit into a box attached to the table. You bid by placing an appropriate card on the table, rather than by voice. A monitor calls out your bid for the benefit of the players on the other side of the screen. (The monitors, I suppose, are selected for their ability to produce a dull monotone.) So vocal inflections are eliminated.

These devices are supposed to do away with any suggestion of the Old Black Magic in the League's most important events. A few players, however, swear that the soul of the game has been taken away, with the psychological and personal elements sterilized by the presence of the screens.

You're playing in the Spingold Semi-finals, and the screens are in use. You are vulnerable, they are not. You hear TWO SPADES (weak) on your left, pass, THREE SPADES on your right. What say you with:

♠ 742
♡ AKJ94
◇ K
♣ KJ72

■ ■ ■

There are times when you have to trust the opponents. RHO's three spades is preemptive. He thinks you can make something. Partner is marked short in spades and should have a few values on this bidding. It is quite true that you hardly have enough to bid a game all by yourself, but the opponents have put you under a lot of pressure and you must strain to get in, lest they steal you blind. So you bid FOUR HEARTS, and try to look like your chief worry is missing slam. (Meanwhile, you give silent thanks for the screens. If you had been able to see partner put on any kind of act at all over two spades, you could hardly justify the four heart bid, which most people would classify as a complete shot in the dark.)

There is a long delay on the other side of the world, and finally, the monitor informs you that LHO has passed and your partner has raised to FIVE HEARTS. Oops. Partner thinks you have a really good hand. You pass quickly, since you don't have whatever it is he needs for six. This is one of the hazards of bidding your partner's cards. He may not have a sense of humor.

The spade King is led against five hearts, and you see:

♠ J5
♡ Q1083
◇ A952
♣ A104
□
♠ 742
♡ AKJ94
◇ K
♣ KJ72

Partner has his bid, so you can't really blame it on him if you go minus on this hand. He really did well not to shoot out six by himself. But next time, he may give you a little more room when you climb in alone at the four level.

RHO overtakes the spade King and fires back a spade to the Queen. The spade ten comes next, and you have to ruff this high, with RHO showing out, as expected. The whole hand depends on a club guess. So your idea is to wait to play that suit, while you try to get some sort of *count*. You play a diamond to the King, and go back to dummy with the heart eight to ruff a diamond high. Both opponents follow to the diamond plays, and both follow to a second trump, won in dummy with the Queen. Now you play the diamond Ace and ruff dummy's last diamond. Both opponents follow. Ready to make your guess in clubs?

■ ■ ■

Your "guess" is a lead-pipe cinch. LHO had six spades, four diamonds, two trumps, and a total of thirteen cards to start with. So there is room in his hand for only one club. You play a club to the Ace and see which club LHO has. If it is not the Queen, you can proceed with a club to your Jack, knowing that it must win.

A voice says "Nicely played." It takes you a second to realize that the disembodied voice is partner's, complimenting you from the other side of the screen.

60

To open the bidding with one of a suit, you need some winners, some defensive values, and a convenient second bid. If you have all these features, it doesn't matter much how many high-card points you have. A hand like:

♠ AJxxxxx
♡ Axxx
♢ xx
♣ —

is a one spade opening for my money. You have everything you need to open.

In the District Playoff of the Grand National Pairs event, you hold this hand as dealer:

♠ Q
♡ A63
♢ KQ32
♣ J7642

Neither side is vulnerable. What is your action?

■ ■ ■

Many players wouldn't dream of passing, but there are cogent arguments the other way. Your suits are ragged and the long cards will be hard to establish. Your intermediates are nonexistent. You have no length in the majors, especially spades. Your defensive strength is borderline. And lastly, there will be rebid problems if you open and receive the likely one spade response. After due consideration, you PASS. Partner opens ONE SPADE in third seat, and you have to think again. Should you respond with a jump, or perhaps in notrump?

■ ■ ■

The same arguments that influenced you not to open should preclude any aggressive notrump responses. You have no ready suit to establish at notrump, and a cheaper response may lead to a more accurate auction. As for jumping in a suit, that would suggest that your hand has suddenly improved because of partner's opening, which is anything but the case. You try a simple response of TWO CLUBS. There is some chance that you may be dropped right there, but only if partner has opened on a dog, and only if he has a tolerance for clubs. If you had *four* bad clubs and another heart, you might prefer to make the slightly distorted two notrump response instead of risking two clubs on such a junky suit.

Sure enough, two clubs is passed out! The heart deuce is led, and partner puts down the dummy with a blush:

♠ K10963
♡ K84
◇ J6
♣ A85
□
♠ Q
♡ A63
◇ KQ32
♣ J7642

It looks like partner is one player who likes to open the bidding on sub-minimum values in third seat. This can work out OK on occasion; you get in a mild preempt and direct a lead. Notice that partner could have passed any response you made comfortably. He has his two quick tricks on defense, and he would like a spade lead if your side winds up defending. (His spade spots are pretty good.) All these conditions must be met before any light hand can be opened in third chair. Otherwise, there is more to lose by opening light than there is to gain.

Playing in two clubs, you note several losers. One spade, one heart, two diamonds, probably two clubs. But you can discard your heart loser on a spade in dummy, and plan to ruff your fourth diamond in dummy. The play will require some care, though. How do you proceed?

■ ■ ■

You win the heart lead in hand, and lead the Queen of spades immediately. You must establish your spade discard early, before the opponents get a chance to lead hearts again, and set up a trick in that suit.

They win the spade Ace on your left and continue hearts. You win in dummy (where you want to be), and take a heart discard on the spade King. Now what?

■ ■ ■

You must go after diamonds next. You plan to ruff your fourth diamond, so you must knock out the diamond Ace while you still have control of the trump suit. You therefore lead the Jack of diamonds to LHO's Ace, and ruff the heart return. Now that you have taken care of all your other business, you can play trumps. But you must not lead out Ace and another. The opponents might win and draw a third round of trumps for you, preventing you from ruffing your diamond loser. So you *duck* the first round of trumps. RHO wins and returns a diamond. You win, and play a trump to your Ace. Both opponents follow, so there is an outstanding high trump, which you can afford to ignore at this point. You ruff a spade, cash your other high diamond, and ruff the last diamond in dummy, letting the opponents score their high trump whenever they want it. Making three clubs.

Notrump, as it happened, made no more than seven tricks at many tables, so +110 proved to be a reasonable score for your pair. And you felt that maybe there was something to this notion of not opening the bidding just because it's your turn.

61

Your partner in the team game this evening is a man who loves to post-mortem the hands right at the table. As soon as the play is over, you'll get to hear a stirring analysis of who could have made what and how it could have been done. I'm sure you have a couple of these types at your own club, since the species seems to be very common. Unfortunately, the worst analysts and the biggest talkers are often one and the same. Usually, the comments are so trite they could have been left unsaid, or else they leave something to be desired in accuracy. Analyzing bridge hands, after all, is a tricky business. I'd be a wealthy man if I had a dime for every authoritative pronouncement I've heard at the table that failed to stand up under close scrutiny in the bar later. And the biggest irony of all is that the most interesting hands are the ones that can receive not even a raised eyebrow. Often, somebody will play an innocent looking dummy and make his contract, unaware that the line of play he chose was inferior. But since it worked, the hand is left blissfully behind, with declarer never suspecting that he just got off with his hide. If you want to improve, you really need to study *all* your results, the good ones as well as the not so good.

This evening provides a rather striking example of what I'm talking about. At IMP scoring, you are dealt:

♠ J53
♡ Q932
◇ KQ83
♣ A3

Your side is vulnerable, the opponents are not. Partner opens ONE HEART and RHO overcalls ONE SPADE. You bid THREE HEARTS, which is forcing with your present partner, and LHO competes with THREE SPADES. Partner now says FOUR DIAMONDS. That might be a slam try, but the way this auction sounds, it is more realistic to expect that partner just wants you to know that he has length and strength in diamonds. That way, he hopes that you will have a better idea what to do when your side faces the inevitable four spade save against your game. As you expect, RHO goes on to FOUR SPADES. What is your action?

■ ■ ■

This is a minimum raise in high cards, but you have a massive fit with partner's second suit. The club Ace will be a good card for offensive purposes, and you have little waste in spades opposite partner's probable singleton. So you decide to bid FIVE HEARTS. You would prefer a double with a hand like:

♠ Kxx
♡ Q9xx
♢ Jxxx
♣ AK

All pass to five hearts, the spade three is led, and partner makes short work of the play.

♠ J53
♡ Q932
♢ KQ83
♣ A3

♠ A
♡ AJ10654
♢ A952
♣ 107

(How would you play the hand if you were declarer?)

■ ■ ■

Partner won the spade Ace, went to the club Ace, and rode the heart Queen, losing to the King. They cashed a club and played another spade, which he ruffed. After drawing the last trump, he tested diamonds with a shrug. When that suit split 3-2, he claimed five. Next hand. Not even any comments, except for a "Nice bid, partner." You took your cards out of the next board with a vague inquisitive feeling gnawing at a back corner of your mind.

Came the comparison of scores, and you found that your five heart bid had gained you eight IMPs. Your teammates were doubled in four spades in the replay, and that contract went for a penalty of only 300. But the vague feeling of doubt stayed around to bug you.

Much later, burning your midnight oil, you discovered the truth. Partner deserved to go down in five hearts. There was a better line than the one he took. If somebody had held J10xx of diamonds, he *would* have gone down. But best play would make the contract even against a bad diamond split, provided trumps were 2-1. (And the opponents could *make* ten tricks at spades if both red suits split very badly.)

Partner should have plunked down his trump Ace at trick two. Say that both opponents follow low. Declarer goes to the club Ace, ruffs a spade, goes to a diamond honor for another spade ruff (eliminating the spades), and gets out of the lead with either a trump or his club loser. The opponents will be unable to extricate themselves. If diamonds are in fact 4-1, the hand that wins will either have to give declarer a ruff-and-discard, or lead from the J10x of diamonds, allowing him to pick up that suit without loss. Try it yourself and see.

The nearby telephone invites. It is very late, but since partner enjoys a good post-mortem so much, perhaps you should call up and share this one with him right now. Enthusiast that he is, he might not want to wait until morning to find out that he misdummied this hand. You might even dampen his ardor for conducting an inquiry after every hand when he's playing.

62

Sitting down for your first match in a Swiss, you find yourself opposed by a pair of the perennial Little Old Ladies. Very old, very benign looking, and generally resembling somebody's greatgrandmother. There is a popular theory that the Little Old Ladies (hereafter referred to as "LOLs") have some strange powers that can somehow mesmerize the expert (who owns far greater technical skills) and produce good results at the expert's expense, as if by magic. Everybody has a host of stories to tell about the times they were "fixed" by a LOL. And the ACBL's *Easy*

Guide to Duplicate Bridge even alleges that LOLs are sometimes able to play with surprising skill, and are actually entitled to more respect than they normally get.

I think I disagree with this bit of hype. The truth is that LOLs are no better or worse than the majority of average bridge players. What really happens is that the expert is sometimes inclined to get lulled into a false sense of security when playing against a LOL. He sees this sweet looking vision setting there, who surely wouldn't harm a fly much less fiendishly dish out zeros, and he expects good results to fall into his lap by the pail. Maybe he even feels a little guilty about trying so hard against so helpless looking an opponent, and he eases up a little. Maybe he gets caught up in the moment and makes a doubtful bid or play he figures will work against the roll-over-and-play-dead opposition. But even the sweetest old thing can cash Aces and Kings; and so, before he knows what hit him, the expert finds himself saddled with a bad result. It's a tough game.

When playing against LOLs, you should expect to do well. But you must *play* well. Give it your best. Your superior technique will win for you if you just give it a chance. Don't play the Little Old Ladies' game. Don't underestimate them. Go after them and try to grind them down. No quarter asked or given.

On the first board of the match, you pick up a tough hand to describe:

♠ 5
♡ AK7
♢ K96542
♣ AK5

You open ONE DIAMOND, and there is a ONE HEART overcall. Partner responds ONE SPADE. Pass by RHO. Your call.

■ ■ ■

There is no ideal rebid. No number of diamonds is exactly right, notrump is premature, and a two heart cue-bid is senseless. Finally, you settle on TWO CLUBS. If you get raised, you can bid notrump safely. (If everyone passes, two clubs may be the best contract, for all you know.) Partner returns to TWO DIAMONDS. Of course, you will bid some more, even after partner's weak preference, and the only question is how many notrump to try. You decide to bid TWO NOTRUMP only, because your long suit is shabby and partner could have taken a preference with only a doubleton diamond. Partner, however, raises you to THREE NOTRUMP, ending the auction.

The heart Queen is led against you, and you see:

♠ AJ1073
♡ 852
◊ Q8
♣ Q84
□
♠ 5
♡ AK7
◊ K96542
♣ AK5

Partner had a tough bid at *his* second turn. Many players would have bid two spades with his cards, but that bid suggests a *six*-card suit. Actually, he has a good hand for play in *your* suits, with his minor-suit Queens and the spade *Ace;* so his "false preference" was probably the best action. At least it gave you a chance to make another descriptive bid.

Plan the play in three notrump.

■ ■ ■

You duck the first heart. You may lose the lead *twice* before the diamonds are established, so you hold up in hearts even with a *double* stopper. If the opponents switch to spades, you will have to finesse dummy's ten, and hope for good luck later; but the LOL on your left is almost certain to continue hearts, and so it proves. You win the second heart, as RHO follows, and now you must decide how to attack diamonds. What should your plan be?

■ ■ ■

If LHO has AJ10 in diamonds, you will go down one, so you don't worry about that possibility. At matchpoints, you might decide to play LHO for Ax in diamonds, leading low to the Queen and ducking completely on the way back. This way, you could make five, for a possible top. At IMPs, though, you want only to make *three*, so your objective is to establish the diamond suit without letting LHO in twice. The crucial cases are when LHO's diamonds are AJx or A10x. If you lead low to the Queen, LHO will remain with two diamond tricks, and will have time to establish hearts and set you. The best play is a low diamond toward dummy, intending to insert the *eight* if LHO follows low. If you can lose a diamond trick to RHO, who has no more hearts at this point, you will be able to set up the suit (against a normal 3–2 break), and gain the timing you need to shut out the heart suit.

63

It happened this way. You were sitting around the club one day in the middle of a hot post-mortem, when all of a sudden, things got just a shade hotter. The front door opens, and in walks a vision of loveliness named Sheila. About 23, five foot four, 110 pounds or so. And with the most extraordinary blue eyes. Sheila had just moved in from out of town and didn't know a soul and had played a little duplicate and had 40 Master Points and was it very hard to get partners around here? Well, you might, just might, be persuaded to sit down opposite Sheila. So here you were in the Friday night game, trying hard to put up flawless technique. It's sure easy to play over your head with those imploring blue eyes across the table spurring you on.

Three quarters of the way through the session, though, there came a vicious test of your ability to keep the wench impressed. First in hand and vulnerable, you held:

♠ AKQ853
♡ KJ5
♢ 4
♣ Q96

You opened ONE SPADE and Sheila, in that soft and cultured voice that really turned you on, bid TWO NOTRUMP. "I am about to make a skip bid," said nasty RHO. "Please simulate intense thought for ten seconds. FOUR CLUBS." You did what you had to, and then bid FOUR SPADES;

and the beautiful Shelia tossed a little smile in your direction and bid *SIX SPADES*. All passed quickly, and LHO led the Ace of hearts, while you awaited dummy with all sorts of hopes and fears.

♠ J102
♡ Q106
◇ AK95
♣ A73
□
♠ AKQ853
♡ KJ5
◇ 4
♣ Q96

You gave it the quick once-over and figured that if you brought *this* one home, you were definitely in tight with Sheila. All followed to the heart Ace, and LHO continued with a heart, on which RHO discarded a high club! You looked up at your partner; and she was still smiling, and that was just as well, because the hand was now an open book for anybody, but especially for you, playing with Sheila. Right? How do you proceed to win the fair maiden?

■ ■ ■

RHO was marked with 0-1-5-7 pattern, and the way to twelve tricks was clear. You won the second heart with the *King*, and ran all of your trumps but one, discarding dummy's little clubs. Finally, you led to the Queen of hearts in this position:

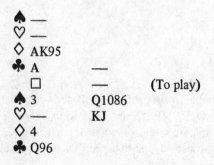

♠ —
♡ —
◇ AK95
♣ A
□   —
♠ 3   Q1086   (To play)
♡ —   KJ
◇ 4
♣ Q96

RHO was stuck. If he pitched a club, you would cash the club Ace and ruff a diamond back to your good clubs. If he pitched a diamond instead, Ace, King, and another diamond would establish dummy's last one, with the club Ace for an entry.

"That was wonderful," Sheila breathed, looking more beautiful than ever. You felt like the lord of all you surveyed. "At least half the credit is yours, my dear," you responded gallantly. "Not only did you make the master bid of six spades, that beautiful winning smile of yours so flustered poor LHO that he failed to break up the squeeze by shifting to a diamond at trick two."

And so it came to pass that you and Sheila went on to wrap up the Friday night game. And you made a date to play next Friday night as well. And after that, who knows? I won't spoil the story by having Sheila turn up with a husband who used to play middle linebacker for the Pittsburgh Steelers, and three children.

64

Your name is ... (please insert your name) ... and you are representing the United States in the World Championship of bridge, the Bermuda Bowl. This is the crucial match, versus the Italian Blue Team (who else?), and Garozzo is on your left, Belladonna on your right. Just for this match, they are playing a natural system, and with nobody vulnerable, Belladonna opens ONE DIAMOND. Your hand is:

♠ AQJ3
♡ 64
◇ 1063
♣ AJ72

You suppress an urge to overcall one spade, and you wind up mentally mopping your brow when Garozzo, to your left, *responds* ONE SPADE. Belladonna raises to TWO SPADES, and this is passed around to your partner, who reopens with a DOUBLE. You might shoot out a pass against anybody else here, but Garozzo has been known to get the most from his dummy play, and letting him declare doubled partials may not be your optimum strategy, at least not when you appear to have a club fit. You cravenly move out to THREE CLUBS.

All pass, Garozzo leads the nine of diamonds, and partner, mumbling that he was hoping he wouldn't have to show the world what he balanced on, puts down:

```
                   ♠ 64
                   ♡ A852
                   ◇ KJ5
                   ♣ K1063
   Garozzo      □      Belladonna
                   ♠ AQJ3
                   ♡ 64
                   ◇ 1063
                   ♣ AJ72
```

It looks like even Garozzo would have had trouble in two spades doubled, and three clubs is no cinch. Belladonna wins the Queen and Ace of diamonds, Garozzo following, and leads a third round which Garozzo ruffs. Then comes a spade, to the King and your Ace. You have an inescapable heart loser, so the contract depends on playing trumps for no losers. How do you go about it?

■ ■ ■

Knowing the distribution of the concealed hands is frequently helpful, as we have seen. If you knew the club distribution here, you could pick up the suit easily. Sometimes, a count of the hand can be obtained by watching the play as it proceeds. But here, the crucial suit is *trumps*, and you cannot delay playing the trump suit while you try to dig up some information about the opponents' distribution. The only safe way to get a count is *inferentially*.

Look. Belladonna had five diamonds, right? And Garozzo had two. The spades were obviously 4–3. Garozzo needed four to bid the suit, and Belladonna couldn't have raised with less than three-card support. How about hearts? Garozzo couldn't have had five. He would have bid them before a four-card spade suit. Matter of fact, if he had four cards in *each* major, he would have bid his suits "up-the-line." But if Garozzo had only two hearts, then Belladonna would have had five, and would have opened one heart.

Starting to get the picture? Garozzo had four spades, three hearts, two diamonds, *four clubs*. You cash the club Ace and lead a club to the ten, winning the trick as Belladonna shows out. Drawing the last trump, you concede a heart, and make your contract exactly. Nicely done. Even Garozzo couldn't have done it better.

65

Your partners have gotten into this annoying habit lately. Whenever the two of you play in an event with a Qualifying session, they never seem to qualify. Of course, *you* always qualify, but for some deep, dark reason, the Conditions of Contest decree that you both have to play in the Consolation (or, as it is better known, the "Goats"). There is definitely no justice. But even in the Goats, you should give it your best effort. That way, you won't have anything to feel sorry about later. And perhaps there may even be a memorable hand or two for you to play. No law against it, even in the Consolation.

After a 136 in the afternoon, you find yourself you-know-where that night. Toward the end of the session, you deal yourself:

♠ J94
♡ J5
♢ AQJ9
♣ AK104

What is your opening bid?

■ ■ ■

Some people might treat this as a club-diamond hand, and open in a suit. But the distribution is balanced, and the minor honors in the majors beg for notrump. So you choose to open ONE NOTRUMP. Partner raises to TWO NOTRUMP. You have average high-card strength and average distribution, but your spot cards are attractive, and the Jacks will pull their full weight at a notrump contract. If your philosophy is to seize a chance for a top score, you will bid THREE NOTRUMP without much thought. You will seldom get a top by taking the conservative view in a situation like this. Even if the game is not particularly a sound one, poor defense may allow nine tricks to be made at many tables. Especially in the Consolation, your best strategy is to go for it.

LHO leads the club five against three notrump, and here's the dummy:

♠ 1063
♡ A104
◇ K106
♣ J862
□
♠ J94
♡ J5
◇ AQJ9
♣ AK104

Not too good. It looks like partner added a point or two for his own spots.

Applying the *Rule of Eleven,* you put in dummy's club six at trick one, expecting it to hold, which it does. (You subtracted *five,* the spot that was led, from *eleven.* The remainder gave the number of cards higher than the five that were held by dummy, RHO, and yourself. Since you and dummy had all six of these cards, you knew that RHO could not beat dummy's six-spot.) So now you are up to eight tricks. Can you see any likely prospects for a ninth one?

■ ■ ■

I can't either, frankly. Your chances of developing another trick by force certainly look slim. You could play LHO for both of the missing heart honors, a 25 percent shot. But with a good heart holding, your LHO might have led a heart instead of a club. Your best chance in a case like this is to abandon the iron of force for the velvet of deceit. At trick two, you lead a *spade* from dummy. RHO plays low, which you like, and you put in your nine with an air of confidence. I once saw the nine hold in this same situation—stranger things have happened—but even if you're unlucky and they win, say, the Queen on your left, your play may pay off. Your LHO's hand is:

♠ AQx
♡ Kxx
◇ xxx
♣ Q9xx

He knows that another club lead will cost, and your spade play smoke-screen has thrown up a psychological barrier to his leading that suit. After thinking for a long time, he shifts to a heart. You play low from dummy, and now it's your RHO who puts on his thinking cap. Finally he plays the nine, from his Q9xxx, and you find yourself the proud pos-sessor of nine tricks!

The guileful spade lead at the second trick also caters to "rectifica-tion of the count" for a possible squeeze, and might cause the opponents to block their spade suit. And there is really no alternative here but to try to get the opponents to help you. There is nothing wrong with giving them a few tricks early if you wind up making nine in the end.

So you didn't win the Consolation. At least your score was a lot better than the one you posted in the afternoon session.

66

Once upon a time, I had a 79 percent game with Norman Kay. I really did, honest. The only sad note: this was in an Individual. And after two hands as my partner Mr. Kay went off to have another 79 percenter with somebody else, while I struggled to score above average with *my* next partner.

There always seems to be an Individual scheduled on the first day of the Nationals, presumably placed there strategically, before the bridge gets more serious and the players settle down to trying to win the Vander-bilt and other life and death matters. It would do just as well or better, I think, to have an Individual on the *last* day of the tournament, when everybody's brain is addled from the ferocious concentration of ten days' tough bridge, and a touch of the ridiculous would do as an outlet. Because that's pretty much what an Individual is. Anything—anything at all—can happen and often does when the pairings are all unfamiliar. Any resemblance to partnership bridge is purely coincidental and the results can sometimes be charitably described as random. Oh, there are the inevitable connoisseurs who delight in getting the most from an unknown partner, and in the other techniques peculiar to an Individual. But most of the players are there because they just feel like playing a little bridge and seeing what happens. As for the real game, that starts tomorrow.

You are playing in an Individual. OK, you are playing in an Individual at gunpoint! (Even if this is your first one and possibly your last one as well, try to enjoy it as long as you're here.) You've never seen your partner before. The first board you await with some trepidation:

♠ Q63
♡ AJ
♢ K863
♣ QJ73

As dealer, you open ONE CLUB. (Angry readers who would prefer one diamond, see hand #27.) Partner responds ONE HEART, and you make your ONE NOTRUMP rebid. Now partner jumps to THREE CLUBS, and you have a small problem. Is that intended as forcing or not? The only clue you have to go on is that your partner is a little old man, about sixty-five years old.

■ ■ ■

Back in the days when everybody played the original Goren style, all of responder's jump preferences and jump rebids were forcing. But now many players use a *limit* style (perhaps influenced by duplicate bridge, where stopping in an accurate part score is just as important as bidding the right game), in which most of responder's secondary jumps are only invitational. To create a forcing situation, these partnerships often have to make a bogus bid in the *fourth suit.* Any regular partnership needs to discuss what style they will play; but you have no such luxury here. The only thing to rely on is partner's age. Since he looks to be over sixty, you decide to assume he is an old fashioned bidder, and has forced you. You try THREE NOTRUMP, hoping for the best. Even if you are wrong, maybe the contract won't be totally hopeless.

All pass, LHO leads the spade seven, and you see that you needn't have worried:

♠ A52
♡ Q642
◇ A2
♣ A1052

□

♠ Q63
♡ AJ
◇ K863
♣ QJ73

Why partner didn't simply raise one notrump to three is a question you'd rather not know the answer to. He's by no means strong enough to consider six clubs. Anyway, RHO plays the spade Jack at trick one, and you win. How do you play from here?

■ ■ ■

You are a big favorite if the club finesse works, but you should not lead clubs right away. Consider what might happen if you took a losing club finesse at the second trick. RHO would return a spade, establishing his partner's suit. With only eight tricks (count 'em), you would have to fall back on the heart finesse, and if it failed as well, LHO would be in to cash his spades. (Instead of taking the heart finesse, you might be able to cash all your minor-suit winners and *endplay* LHO with your last spade; but this is not a guaranteed line.)

A superior plan is to play hearts early, attacking the potential entry to the dangerous spade suit. But it is slightly dangerous to lead out Ace and Jack of hearts. If RHO happened to have six hearts (about a 5 percent shot, maybe more with LHO holding spade length), he could win and return a heart, placing you in some hot water. Nor is it safe for you to go to dummy with the diamond Ace and lead a heart to your Jack. The opponents might win and continue diamonds, setting up five tricks. The only safe play is to lead your Jack of hearts at trick two. If it holds, you can switch to clubs in comfort (leading *low* to the ten first, in case LHO has the bare King). If they win the first heart and continue spades, you can hold up, win the third spade, and take the club finesse, hoping for RHO to be out of spades if he wins.

67

Back in the Thirties and Forties, there were a lot fewer bridge tournaments, and Master Points were dearly won. Even victory in a National Championship might get you only a few of them. But inflation has hit the bridge world like everything else. Now, there is a tournament within driving distance almost every weekend unless you live in Nova Scotia, and the Master Point awards for winning are incomparably larger. Among the players who attend tournaments regularly, I would estimate that perhaps three quarters are Life Masters; and almost everybody who can play this game at all has over *50* Master Points.

It used to be realistic to have concurrent Masters' and Non-Masters' Pairs events, with the dividing line being 50 or 100 Points, but no longer. The idea I'm leading up to is that there should be *lots more events for Life Masters.* Most players never get to play in a Life Masters' event, except at the Nationals, and given the present state of things, that seems ridiculous. The "flighted" events that are now a part of many tournaments have helped some, but surely it's time for the "Masters" Pairs to go the way of all flesh. Think how much more fun and prestige there would be to winning a Life Masters' Pairs!

Sorry about my diatribe. Back to the hands. Your club decided to hold a special two-session event for Life Masters only. After easing along over average for the best part of the first session, you meet this hand:

♠ K8
♡ KQ862
♢ 4
♣ KJ953

You open ONE HEART. Partner thinks for a while and responds TWO DIAMONDS. What do you do now?

■ ■ ■

Right, you have to rebid TWO HEARTS, since a three club rebid would suggest a lot more high-card strength than you possess. Next you hear TWO SPADES from partner. What is *your* next action?

■ ■ ■

If you rebid three clubs now, partner may think you are 6-4; but it looks even stranger to bid notrump with this pattern. So you trot out your other suit. THREE CLUBS. THREE HEARTS from partner. That must be forcing; he would have raised your two heart rebid to three hearts (or made some other bid that would have limited his hand earlier) if he had only invitational strength. But he could have only two hearts, or three small ones, so you bid THREE NOTRUMP with your good clubs. Partner takes you back to FOUR HEARTS, however, and you pass gratefully.

The opening lead is a low spade, and muttering that he hopes you don't make too many, partner puts down:

♠ Q942
♡ A53
♢ AQJ1073
♣ —
□
♠ K8
♡ KQ862
♢ 4
♣ KJ953

You play low from dummy on the opening lead, and RHO flinches and puts in the Jack. You win the King. Where do you go from here?

■ ■ ■

The diamond suit will be your main source of tricks, and the best way to hit diamonds is with a *ruffing finesse*. You lead a diamond to the Ace, and then call for the diamond Queen. You plan to discard your losing spade if this isn't covered. You have less to lose by playing the diamond suit this way (instead of leading a diamond to the ten), and you have a suspicion that the diamond King is on your right anyway. Without that card, RHO wouldn't have been as likely to risk ducking the first trick.

The ruffing finesse works like a charm for you, LHO following with a small diamond, so you continue with the diamond Jack from dummy. This time RHO plays the King, you ruff with the heart six, and LHO follows. At this point, you can draw three rounds of trumps ending in dummy, and, if the trumps have split, run the diamonds for eleven tricks. Can you see anything better to do?

■ ■ ■

In fact, you might do better by drawing only *two* rounds of trumps, with the King and Ace, then starting on diamonds. You can always wind up using dummy's last trump to ruff a club, thus recovering the trick you lose by leaving a trump outstanding. And what will the opponents do when one of them ruffs in with that last trump? Suppose that LHO has it. He will have to get out with a black suit. On a spade lead, you will play dummy's nine, hoping to force out the Ace and establish a trick with the Queen. If LHO leads a club, you will discard from dummy, hoping that your King will win.

LHO's hand was:

♠ 10xxx
♡ Jxx
♦ xxx
♣ A10x

The recommended line would earn you a precious second overtrick, which should be worth a top, even in a field of Life Masters.

Facing a pair of Florida experts in the Grand National Teams Zonal Playoff, you lurk in third chair with:

♠ A4
♡ K87542
♦ AJ53
♣ Q

After two passes, you open ONE HEART, and receive a raise to TWO HEARTS. Both sides are vulnerable. Do you feel like bidding any more?

■ ■ ■

It must be right to bid, since a valuable vulnerable game could be close to laydown opposite as little as:

♠ xxxx
♡ AJxx
◇ xx
♣ xxx

But if partner's trump support is mediocre, then game could be shaky even if his overall strength is good, e.g.:

♠ Kxx
♡ xxx
◇ Qxx
♣ KJxx

Your best game try is a simple reraise to THREE HEARTS. Partner will base his decision on general strength, but will pay special attention to the quality of his trumps if the decision is close. (Some pairs like to play a reraise here as *preemptive;* luckily, your pair isn't one of them.)

After due consideration, partner puts you in FOUR HEARTS and all pass. A low club is led, and partner shrugs at you and puts down:

♠ 97532
♡ AQ6
◇ Q4
♣ 975
□
♠ A4
♡ K87542
◇ AJ53
♣ Q

The club Ace wins to your right, and the club Jack is returned. You ruff low, and LHO follows. You play a heart to dummy, all following, and lead the diamond Queen. The King covers on your right and you win the Ace. Things have gone smoothly so far. But how do you play from here on?

■ ■ ■

You have nine sure tricks and you will try to nail down the tenth one by taking a diamond ruff in dummy. Should you draw another round of trumps at this point? No, if RHO had three trumps and could overruff the dummy on the third diamond, there would be no further chance for a tenth trick. How about ruffing a diamond low right now? That's risky too. RHO might overruff and produce the last outstanding trump, leaving you stuck with a diamond loser.

The only really safe way to ten tricks is to ruff the third diamond with a high trump, ruff a club back to hand, and then lead your last diamond and try to ruff it. No matter what the opponents do, you will come to ten tricks. If the fourth diamond is overruffed, you will be able to draw the other trump, and make all six of your trumps in hand, two diamonds, a spade, and a ruff in dummy. If they do not overruff the fourth diamond, you may wind up losing a trump trick, but the extra diamond ruff will compensate.

Note, as a tailpiece, partner's raise to two hearts in lieu of a one spade response. He made the bid that limited and described his values immediately. Maybe the next stop for the two of you will be the Nationals!

69

If you were to ask the average bridge player how he got started at the game, chances are he would say he picked it up on campus. I teach a little bridge, and sometimes I feel like half my life is being spent trying to salvage housewives who "learned a little bridge in college." Not that learning bridge in college is necessarily a bad thing. I started learning there myself, usually when I should have been concentrating on nobler pursuits, like memorizing the poetry of some forgotten bard or sweating down the declension of Latin nouns.

Our best bridge games always started at the beginning of Final Exams (and sometimes lasted for the duration, with unavoidable breaks; looking back, it seems like there were times when I rushed off to take an exam when I was dummy). Once my group even came up with a magnificent plan to approach the Administration about offering bridge classes for academic credit. Our main justification was that we spent more time on bridge than anything else anyhow. Even now that I am older and certain childish notions have been dismissed, I still think this wouldn't be a bad idea. As Terence Reese once wrote, bridge teaches more about life than many of the courses that *are* offered for credit in a stuffy curriculum.

I never expect to see this beautiful logic accepted by the educational powers that be, though.

Returning for a moment to the golden days of yore, you are playing in a fraternity house game when you ought to be studying. Your hand is:

♠ 53
♡ AJ642
◇ AK73
♣ 102

Partner takes a swig from his beer and opens ONE NOTRUMP (sixteen-eighteen). You respond THREE HEARTS, forcing to game and asking him to support your suit if possible. But partner introduces FOUR CLUBS. What do you make of that?

■ ■ ■

Partner would return to notrump on any hand without heart support, so four clubs equals hearts! He has an excellent heart fit and a maximum hand, and has shown a concentration of values in case you think slam is possible. This is called an "advance cue-bid," because it is a cue-bid made when a trump suit is agreed on only by implication. You can certainly cue-bid FOUR DIAMONDS in reply. This excites partner even more, since he Blackwoods, and jams it into SIX HEARTS when you show two Aces. He must have a rock.

The opening lead is a trump, and you see that partner may have had one beer too many:

♠ KQ82
♡ K103
◇ Q5
♣ AK74
□
♠ 53
♡ AJ642
◇ AK73
♣ 102

Partner's bidding is questionable at best. His launching into Blackwood was a case of rebidding the same values he had already shown you once.

Having overstated his heart fit with the four club bid, he should surely have signed off at four hearts over your four diamonds, and left any further slam moves up to you. Even if you had tried for slam again (with five diamonds), it is doubtful if he should accept. You could bid five *hearts* over four hearts if *all* you needed for slam at that point was a control in the unbid suit. Notice that slam would be slightly above average if partner just had a fourth heart.

Back to the play. This trump lead seems helpful. How do you proceed?

■ ■ ■

You appear to have five heart tricks (no hope for you if there is a trump loser), three diamonds, and two clubs on top, and at least one more trick is available in spades. You could look for your twelfth trick by leading up to the spade honors twice, but this is only a 50-50 chance at best (LHO might have *led* the spade Ace if he had it). A better chance is to try for a diamond ruff in dummy. But if you choose that line, this can be an easy hand to lose at trick one. You need to play the heart *King* from dummy on the first trick. If RHO has the singleton Queen of hearts, you must save dummy's low trump to ruff with, since ruffing with an honor will set up a trick for LHO's 98xx. If RHO follows low, you can always finesse him for the Queen later. This is safe, because no LHO would lead away from the Queen of trumps against a slam.

On the heart King, justice is served, for once, as the Queen falls on your right. Now, should you take your diamond ruff immediately?

■ ■ ■

It wouldn't be advisable to do so, with the trumps 4-1. If you ruff a diamond now, you will either have to (1) ruff a club back to hand to draw trumps later, in which case you will be out of control, and the opponents might be able to cash a club trick when you try to set up a spade for your twelfth trick; or, (2) if you lead a spade honor after taking your ruff, you may find that LHO had 2-4-2-5 pattern. He would discard a spade on the third diamond and be able to ruff a second round of spades for the setting trick.

You had better lead the King of spades at trick *two*. RHO wins the Ace and returns a spade. LHO plays the Jack, and dummy wins. You continue with the Queen, Ace, and a low diamond. LHO discards a spade, and dummy ruffs low. After cashing the ten of hearts, you have only to guess how to get safely back to your hand to draw trumps. Should you try to ruff a club or a spade?

■ ■ ■

The reasoning you came up with was a little convoluted. LHO had two diamonds, four hearts, and at least three spades. If he had exactly three spades to begin with, he would defend as he actually had. If he had four spades and three clubs originally, anything you tried would work. If LHO started with five or six spades, you needed to lead a spade at this point; but with only one or two clubs, LHO would probably have made the natural play of discarding a club earlier. So you played three rounds of clubs, ruffing. LHO followed, to your relief, and you were able to finish getting in the trumps and make your improbable slam.

Then, as you were writing down the score, it occurred to you that, if LHO *had* held two clubs and five spades, it would have been a good deceptive defense for him to pitch a *spade* on the third diamond. He would have induced you to try to get back to your hand with a club ruff. Perhaps your convoluted logic was a little shaky. You sensed that bridge, with all its subtleties, was getting to be a little too demanding of you. Maybe you should spend more time on some of your easier subjects, like Topology.

70

You sat down to play in the Open that day with a good partner, a very good partner. And things went well, very well. They started beautifully and got better. The two of you made few errors, and none that were at all costly, while the opponents stubbed their toes a few times. You got the maximum from your own hands, your opposition fell down on some of theirs. You were definitely on a roll.

There may be such a thing as *momentum* in a Pairs' game. Sometimes, you can get this strange, peaceful feeling that you will do well even if your next opponents turn out to be Forquet and Garozzo. And so it was that day. After the ninth round, you idly picked up your Convention Card and looked up and down the row of scores. Partner said later that your eyes got sort of big. Your Card showed eighteen plus scores and no minuses. The bridge equivalent to pitching a no hit game! Both of you knew what was happening, but nobody dared say anything about it.

Came the tenth round, with the pressure now starting to build. The opponents were familiar to you, and you would have rather seen Barry Crane and Company come to the table. This is another funny thing about playing duplicate bridge. There will always be certain pairs that you absolutely *own*. They couldn't score a single matchpoint against you if you played them from dawn to dusk. And then, inevitably, there are the pairs who kill *you* every time you sit down against them. You may be much the better pair on paper, but they eat you alive, nevertheless. Nobody could ever explain why this should be true, but it is. I know. As for your present opposition, you happen to be their favorite pigeon.

The opponents go down in three notrump on the first board, amazingly enough, so your streak is still alive. But the second board puts you in some definitely hot water. To begin with, you pick up an unbiddable hand:

♠ 5
♡ KQ96
♢ K62
♣ AKJ73

There are three passes to you. What are your plans? (Remember that you will have to find a rebid over partner's likely spade response.)

■ ■ ■

If you open one club and hear the dreaded one spade, you will have to overbid (two hearts) or underbid (one notrump, two clubs) at your second turn. So you prefer a ONE HEART opening, hoping to avoid having to "reverse" on shaded values or otherwise distort your hand. If partner responds one spade or one notrump, you can bid an economical two clubs next. If he responds two diamonds, you can bid three clubs safely; since partner's two-level response suggests a decent hand, nothing bad is likely to happen to you.

An expert plans his second bid as a routine part of choosing an opening bid. Planning a little *further* ahead, if the bidding goes: one heart; one spade; two clubs; and partner now takes a heart preference (maybe on only a doubleton heart), you are good enough to bid a third time, trying for game even in the face of partner's announced weakness. You would bid two notrump, and partner would not insist on hearts unless he had real support. Considering this discussion, you can see how selecting an opening bid with an eye to how the subsequent bidding may develop is an important skill in the auction.

Anyway, you open one heart, get the expected ONE SPADE response, and follow through with TWO CLUBS. Over that, partner jumps to THREE HEARTS. He shows invitational values, and you have enough to accept easily; but you have to bid THREE NOTRUMP, since partner probably has only three-card heart support for his delayed raise. However, partner takes you back to FOUR HEARTS over three notrump, so you pass, hoping he knows what he's doing.

The diamond ten is led, and the dummy is disappointing:

  ♠ KQ962
  ♡ 8742
  ◇ Q5
  ♣ Q10
    □
  ♠ 5
  ♡ KQ96
  ◇ K62
  ♣ AKJ73

Partner's one spade could have worked well, since you might have held:

  ♠ AJ10
  ♡ AKxxx
  ◇ KJ10x
  ♣ x

or some similar hands where spades could make more tricks than hearts. A more delicate question is whether his hand is worth a game invitational sequence at all. His Queens are devalued for suit play, and his spade honors may be wasted opposite a heart-club two-suiter. His lack of a heart honor is a bad sign.

It looks as though you may lose four tricks. RHO fires up with the Ace of diamonds at trick one, and returns a diamond to the Queen. Plan the play from here.

■ ■ ■

It seems like there is no reason to delay playing trumps, hoping for a 3–2 split with the Ace onside. But suppose you take your time. Lead the spade King from dummy at trick three. This is won on your right and another diamond comes back, your King taking. What do you think the right play in trumps is now?

■ ■ ■

As you no doubt realize, it cannot be right to play for the Ace onside now. RHO passed in third seat and has shown up with two Aces and the diamond Jack, so LHO must have the Ace of trumps. Your only chance is to play for the Jack-ten onside. So you go over to dummy with a club to lead the eight of hearts and pass it. (Really, you could have ruffed your good King of diamonds to get to the dummy.)

Alas, the eight of hearts lost to the ten, and you went down a trick. But at least you gave it your best shot and partner praised your technique. Better that than having to explain to him why you missed the best play when it would have worked. As for your no-hitter, well, they just singled up the middle against you, Fernando. Maybe at your next turn in the rotation.

part three

FOR YOU, THE EXPERT

71

I think that the single greatest thing about tournament bridge is that you may sit down to play and find yourself opposed by a World Champion! I like to play golf, but I never expect to go up against Nicklaus or Tom Watson. Tournament bridge is different. There are plenty of events in which even the most inexperienced but ebullient tyro may get to tee it up against the best we have to offer.

This hand is from a Regional Mens' Pairs. The facts of life being that most of the better players are men, this is a tough game. It usually takes a lower score to win the Mens' Pairs than the Womens' Pairs, which is held at the same time. You sit down to play at table 3 (where the top-seeded pair in your section is assigned), and your LHO looks suspiciously like Bob Hamman. A surreptitious check of the opponents' Convention Card reveals that he really *is* Bob Hamman. You deal, and hold:

♠ AKQ86
♡ 1072
◇ A63
♣ K5

What is your opening bid?

■ ■ ■

This is a classic dilemma. One spade or one notrump? There are a hundred more or less cogent arguments on both sides of the question.

("You should open one notrump with your *running* spade suit. If your suit were ragged, you might need time to establish it, time that might not be available in notrump." "Yes, but if you have *bad* spades and your strength is concentrated elsewhere, wouldn't *that* be a more logical time to open in notrump?" Etc.)

Can anyone claim to know the right answer? Personally, I hate to pass up a chance to convey the strength and approximate distribution of my hand with one bid. I can relax from then on, and let partner do the worrying. I'll impose a ONE NOTRUMP opening bid on you here.

Partner raises you to THREE NOTRUMP, and Hamman leads the six of clubs. You see:

♠ 1052
♡ AQ96
◇ K94
♣ QJ4
□
♠ AKQ86
♡ 1072
◇ A63
♣ K5

You win the first trick with the club King, and test the spades by leading the King and Queen. On the second round, the Jack falls on your right. Now you lead the seven of hearts to dummy's nine. This play has nothing to lose, and might let you make six if both heart honors are well placed. The Jack wins to your right, and back comes a club. Low from Hamman. Dummy's Jack wins. You still have a chance to make six. You come to hand with a spade and lead a second heart toward dummy. Low from Hamman. Should you take the second heart finesse (which is, *a priori*, 76 percent to succeed)?

■ ■ ■

The answer: no, you shouldn't, not if your LHO is a World Champion. Hamman knows your whole hand at this point. He knows you have five spade tricks, two diamonds (you need the diamond Ace to fill out your one notrump opening), and two clubs. He knows you have the heart ten from his partner's play of the Jack. If Hamman had the heart King guarded two or three times, he would *never* duck the second club and give you a free chance to make six when he could have held you. You go up with the heart Ace, and the *King falls* on your right. You wind up making six the hard way.

One of the skills involved in good declarer play is drawing inferences from the opening lead and the defenders' play thereafter. If you are lucky enough to have an opponent who can be trusted implicitly to play well, then such inferences, even the most subtle ones, are valid indeed.

72

Your partner has opened the bidding and RHO has doubled for takeout. In choosing an action, keep these points in mind:

1. The auction will often turn competitive, and your side will then have to judge where and how high to compete. Giving partner a reasonably clear description of your hand early may help him to make an accurate decision.

2. There is less reason for you to mention a four-card major suit, particularly a weak one, as you would have done if RHO had passed. RHO should have support for all the other suits, including yours, so that a fit with partner is less likely. Even if there *is* a fit, the play may not go well if RHO has a stout trump holding. (You should be more willing to suppress a shaky four-card *heart* suit, than a mediocre four-bagger in *spades*, the ranking suit.)

As far as the philosophy that you should "ignore the double" and "bid naturally" goes, you might as well ignore a loaded gun pointed at your head!

Playing in a Regional Knockout Teams, your semi-final match pits you against the number one-seeded team. These are all fine players, aggressive and imaginative at the table. You have a lot to gain by winning this match. Toward the end of the first half, you hold this hand:

♠ 9742
♡ K643
♢ A105
♣ Q4

Nobody is vulnerable, and there are three passes around to your partner, who opens up ONE CLUB. RHO now backs in with a DOUBLE. What is your action?

■ ■ ■

The rationale from points (1) and (2) above is especially pertinent at IMP scoring, so you bid a descriptive ONE NOTRUMP. LHO passes, and partner tanks and comes up with TWO NOTRUMP. You have plenty enough to go on to THREE NOTRUMP.

Nobody doubles, and LHO after a brief huddle of his own, puts down the heart ten:

♠ A10
♡ J82
♦ QJ93
♣ AK106
□
♠ 9742
♡ K643
♦ A105
♣ Q4

Since you are not vulnerable, partner's raise was a little hungry. But you told him he could always add a point for your declarer play, so you can't blame him too much. Go ahead and think about the play.

■ ■ ■

Your first move is to cover the heart ten with dummy's Jack. This stands to gain if LHO led a heart from the 107 doubleton. RHO wins the heart Ace and returns the Queen. You win your King, and LHO pauses for several seconds and pitches a club! That was some lead your LHO made. He thought his partner was likely to have five hearts since your side made no effort to get to a heart contract.

Even so, you look like a favorite to make three notrump. You have eight sure tricks and additional chances in the minor suits. First, you want to go to dummy and finesse in diamonds, but the entry situation is such that you must play some clubs to begin with. Now, the best play for four club tricks with this combination of cards is to finesse the ten on the second round, and that play becomes even more attractive with RHO thought to be short in clubs after his takeout double. You get the club Queen out of the way and play your small club toward dummy. Low on your left. Should you take a chance and hook the ten?

■ ■ ■

You will be down if the club finesse loses, and if the diamonds are going to produce four tricks, you don't need the whole club suit anyway. Will the diamond finesse work? Probably not. RHO, a passed hand, has the Ace and Queen of hearts and is likely to have a couple of the missing spade honors as well—perhaps the opening lead would have been a spade if LHO had had a good holding there. So maybe you need to finesse in clubs, taking your best chance for four tricks. You are about to call for the club ten when a nagging doubt surfaces. LHO's club discard. That looks like length in clubs all right—players reflexively discard the "worthless fifth" (or sixth) card in a suit the first time they have to pitch something. But why should LHO think for a little while, and then graciously tell you he has a lot of clubs, especially when he could surely have thrown a non-committal diamond instead? Your LHO is a true expert, remember.

Finally, you call for the club Ace, and the *Jack falls* on your right. You mentally wipe your forehead and silently congratulate LHO on his subtlety. It looks like you are safe now. You lead the diamond Queen and pass it, and it holds. Are you about to make a million? You call for the three of diamonds and play your ten. LHO slaps down the King and returns a spade, and you must win. Suddenly, you see a snag. The diamonds are blocked, and there is no further entry to dummy! Have you blown it?

■ ■ ■

Of course not. Don't panic. You only need to cash your high clubs and discard the blocking diamond Ace. Then you can take your other two diamond tricks, and score up the game. Whew. Negotiating all the pitfalls of a hand like that one should automatically be worth 10 Master Points, shouldn't it?

By the way, you gained 11 IMPs. At the other table, they bid one heart over the takeout double with your cards. You partner's hand decided to raise to two hearts, and there they rested. The contract was an unhappy one and wound up down two. At this rate, you might get to play in the Finals!

73

In tournament bridge, the use of *conventions* has proliferated over the past two decades. A convention is a bid which expert theorists have found expedient to assign some artificial meaning. Take the Unusual Notrump, for example. If your partnership has decided to use this convention (and very few pairs do without it). then a two notrump overcall of the opponents' one-of-a-suit opening says nothing whatever about overcaller's interest in playing the hand at notrump. It has an *un*natural meaning instead, sort of like a message in code. The practitioners of this (and any other) convention believe that the *natural* use of a two notrump overcall in this situation is expendable.

A *treatment,* on the other hand, is a particular way of assigning a natural meaning to a bid. If you and I play a one notrump opening that shows four hearts, six clubs, and fewer than eight high-card points, that's a convention. Very strange (and probably illegal in tournament play), but a convention just the same. But if you and I decide that our one notrump opening will promise a balanced hand with, say, fourteen-sixteen HCP, that is a treatment. We haven't distorted the natural meaning of the notrump opening; we've only chosen the point-count range that we prefer for it.

In the old Goren style, a one notrump opening showed sixteen-eighteen points in high cards. But nowadays, the majority of tournament players probably use a fifteen-seventeen point notrump. There is a reason for this. In tournament bridge, with matchpoint scoring, balanced twelve-point hands are frequently opened. At Pairs, making a part score can conceivably get you a good board as easily as scoring up a grand slam. Since you don't want to miss out on a thing, you are inclined to open a little lighter than at rubber bridge or IMPs, where bidding games and avoiding disasters are the chief goals.

Problems arise if your opening of one of a suit, followed by a *rebid* in notrump, can have a *four*-point range. Accuracy is a lot more difficult, and this is a common bidding sequence in which it is important to be accurate. If you play a one notrump opening to show *fifteen–seventeen* HCP, then a suit opening followed by a notrump rebid can be used to show twelve-*fourteen* HCP, a *narrower* range, and a better scheme for accuracy.

Playing fifteen-seventeen notrumps in a local club game (I did convince you, right?), you pick up:

♠ K5
♡ AK8
◇ Q1042
♣ K652

Over your ONE NOTRUMP opening, partner uses Stayman, and puts you into THREE NOTRUMP when you deny possession of a major suit. A club is led against you, the seven, to be exact, and you see this dummy:

♠ A1042
♡ 7542
◇ AK7
♣ 94
□
♠ K5
♡ AK8
◇ Q1042
♣ K652

RHO wins the club Ace at trick one, and returns the ten. Say you win. Plan the play from here.

■　■　■

Most players would test diamonds right off, and make or fail depending on how the bridge gods had distributed that suit. But you're more patient. You will make nine tricks at most, and LHO is known to have no more than five clubs; so you exit with a club and let LHO take his tricks. Perhaps something favorable will turn up as you watch the discards. At the very least, your chances of playing the diamonds for four tricks may be better later than they are now.

On the third club, dummy throws a heart and RHO throws a heart. On the fourth club, dummy throws a heart and RHO throws a heart. On the fifth club, dummy throws a spade and RHO throws a spade. You discard a spade from hand on the fifth club.

Now comes a middle spade from LHO. Low from dummy, nine on your right, you win your King. You cash your high hearts. RHO plays the heart Queen under your Ace, and discards a spade on the heart King. Both opponents follow low to the Ace and King of diamonds, and on the Ace of spades, RHO plays the Jack, and LHO a small spade. You discard your last heart.

With two tricks to go, dummy has the spade ten and a diamond left. You have the Queen-ten of diamonds. The other missing cards are the Jack and a small diamond, the spade Queen, and the heart Jack. When you lead the diamond from dummy, the last small diamond shows up on your right. Does RHO have the Jack left as well?

■ ■ ■

This is not a difficult problem if you are a master of the subtle inference. RHO started with two clubs and three hearts. Suppose he had three diamonds and five spades. What do you suppose his first discard on the clubs would have been? What would *yours* have been if you had held his cards? Almost certainly, a spade. *Not* a heart from the Qxx, I'll bet.

The fifth card in a suit, the "idle fifth" as it is sometimes called, is always an attractive discard (although it may, as you see, give away some valuable information). RHO is much more likely to have had four spades and four diamonds, so the finesse of the diamond ten is a heavy favorite. The full deal is:

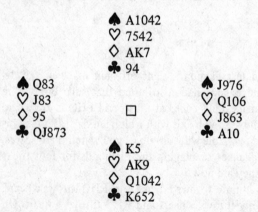

Look at RHO's hand and imagine how you would have discarded in his place. Then imagine how you would have discarded with:

♠ QJ9xx
♡ Qxx
♢ xxx
♣ A10

I think you'll see what I'm talking about.

(There is one other small clue to RHO's hand. If he were down to the Queen-Jack of spades in the end-game, he might have followed to your spade Ace with the *Queen*. This is an application of the Principle of Restricted Choice, which we will hear more about in hand #77.)

74

In a matchpoint duplicate event, the idea is to outscore the other pairs who hold exactly the same cards as you, under an identical set of conditions. (It doesn't matter *how much* you beat them by; 10 points is good enough; your aim is to beat *as many* of your competitors as possible.) In a local club game, there might be ten tables in play, so a good score, about 60 percent of the available matchpoints, would be needed to win. But in a large tournament, there will be several *hundred* pairs in the game. To win in a field that large, you will need a very big score, perhaps over 65 percent.

At matchpoints, your score depends a great deal on how well your opponents play against you, and no pair can avoid the occasional bad board when their opponents do something good or lucky. (If you have too many results like this, you can just resign yourself to waiting for another day.) All this means that, *on your own hands,* the ones on which *you* have the most to say about what your score will be, you must go all out to score the maximum. Fortune definitely favors the bold, and you cannot hope to be successful without seizing whatever opportunities fate deals you.

Playing in the National Open Pairs, which can run to six or seven hundred *tables* (so big it is practically like a lottery), you pick up a promising hand, promsing in the hands of a good matchpoint player, anyway:

♠ K
♡ J4
◊ A83
♣ AKQ10752

You open ONE CLUB. Some pairs play a "Gambling" three notrump opening, and would use it on this hand. Such an opening conventionally shows a long, solid minor suit that will produce most of the tricks needed to make three notrump. Other pairs use the bid, but require less strength outside the long suit than this. Personally, I like to play that a Gambling three notrump opening shows a solid seven-card minor, and nothing else at all. If opener can have a lot of unknown outside strength, accuracy becomes nearly impossible if responder happens to have a good hand, and a slam may be missed.

Over your one club, LHO overcalls ONE SPADE, and this is passed back around to you. What is your action?

■ ■ ■

This is the time to show a little enterprise. Partner is marked with a few scattered points, or else he must have something in spades, judging from the opponents' failure to bid more strongly. Either way, you should be willing to gamble out THREE NOTRUMP(!) at matchpoints. I know you don't have a spade stopper ... well, actually, you do have one, in a way. Put yourself in LHO's shoes. Would *you* lay down the spade Ace against three notrump? He won't either. Almost invariably, you will get the lead of another suit, or a low spade away from the Ace. (The spade King could be your ninth trick.)

All pass to three notrump and the opening lead is a low spade. The dummy is a sight to gladden your heart, provided RHO doesn't play the Ace of spades:

♠ 1084
♡ A9652
◊ Q74
♣ 43
      □
♠ K
♡ J4
◊ A83
♣ AKQ10752

Luckily, RHO can only put up the spade Jack at trick one, and you impassively win your stiff King. Both opponents follow to a high club, so you hit them with six more rounds, closely observing the discards. LHO, who had a singleton club, has to make six pitches. He lets go of two low diamonds, then three spades, then a low heart. RHO, with three clubs to the Jack, must discard four times. His first pitch is the deuce of diamonds, then a middle-sized heart, then a spade, and finally another diamond. The position is now:

♠ 10
♡ A9
♢ Q7
♣ —
□
♠ —
♡ J4
♢ A83
♣ —

You lead a heart to the Ace, with LHO playing the King, and RHO a lower heart than the one he discarded before. Where do you go from here?

■ ■ ■

LHO probably had a six-card spade suit. RHO let go of one spade but not two, and that looks like an original three-card holding in his partner's suit. (If LHO did have only five spades, he is now down to the bare Ace.) Could LHO have the heart Queen and the bare King of diamonds left? That would make RHO's heart plays a little strange. Most defenders tend to give their partner honest information in these situations. Your RHO could be the world's most subtle defender, but chances are he discarded honestly, trying to tell his partner it was safe to unguard hearts. Also, with three small hearts, RHO might have discarded all his hearts early. And, it occurs to you, LHO might have pitched his low heart *early* from KQx. And with the King-Queen of hearts left, LHO might have played his *Queen,* not his King, on your heart lead. There are always a lot of small indications, you can see.

To repeat, the opponents could be doing something diabolical; but you shouldn't discount the obvious to cater to the esoteric. The most likely development is that LHO is down to the Ace-Queen of spades and the King and a small diamond. So you go out dummy's last spade and endplay him. He can cash another spade, but then he has to lead away from his King of diamonds, and you make five notrump.

Perhaps LHO *should* have laid down his Ace of spades—from this hand:

♠ AQ9xxx
♡ Kx
♢ K10xx
♣ x

His lead of a low spade to keep communication was questionable when he had a good hand and his partner was unlikely to ever win a trick. It was *dangerous* to underlead as well, because you were marked with a long suit on the bidding, and a low spade lead could give up a crucial trick, or, as actually happened, expose him to an endplay later.

Anyway, your two overtricks were worth a resounding top, even in a field this large. A few more of these, and you might get your name on the leader board.

75

Somehow, you made it to the Finals of the Life Masters' Pairs in Boston. And the problems start right away. Round one, board two. You wait patiently in fourth seat with:

♠ Q962
♡ Q104
♢ KQ9
♣ K64

Your side only is vulnerable. LHO passes and partner opens ONE CLUB. There is a ONE DIAMOND overcall, described on the opponents' Card as "occasionally light." Should you plan to drive this hand to game? You probably should with a twelve-count plus good intermediates. Your diamond honors look well placed, also. What should you bid at your first turn?

■ ■ ■

A two notrump response here would only be invitational, so your options are to go slow with one spade, planning to bid three notrump at your next turn even if partner raises spades; or, you can just bid three notrump straightaway and let the spade suit go. Your hand is flat as a pancake, your values are all secondary, and you are not interested in hearing partner insist on four spades when he is looking at a singleton diamond. So you just leap to THREE NOTRUMP, hoping for the best.

Partner passes, but his brow is wrinkled as the diamond ten is led against this contract, leading you to believe you may have done the wrong thing.

♠ 3
♡ AJ63
◇ 63
♣ AJ10752
□
♠ Q962
♡ Q104
◇ KQ9
♣ K64

You've seen more robust opening bids. RHO puts on the diamond Ace at trick one. Plan your play.

■ ■ ■

Since you would like a diamond continuation a lot more than a spade shift, you drop your *Queen* of diamonds on the first trick. You still have a tenace left. RHO frowns, but eventually, he leads another diamond, and your nine wins. What is your next play?

■ ■ ■

You would like to postpone the crucial club guess for a while. So you lead your Queen of hearts at trick three. If LHO ducks this without pain, you will go up with dummy's Ace and make your best guess in clubs. As it is, LHO covers the heart Queen, and you take two more hearts, finding that the suit splits evenly. On the fourth heart, RHO throws a diamond, LHO a spade. You come to the club King, both opponents playing small, and cash your high diamond. LHO pitches another spade.

Now a club toward dummy. LHO follows low. This is the big moment. What do you do?

■ ■ ■

With RHO known to have nine red cards and LHO only five, the mathematical odds favor a finesse of the club Jack. But there is an additional indication in favor of the finesse as well. LHO probably has one of the high spades. If RHO had both of them, he would probably have laid down the spade King at trick two to see his partner's reaction, holding a switch back to diamonds in reserve. Now give LHO only two clubs, and therefore *six* spades. His hand would look something like:

♠ KJxxxx (AJxxxx)
♥ Kxx
♦ 10x
♣ xx

That hand might have opened a weak two spades, especially with the vulnerability favorable. So it looks better to play LHO for five spades and three clubs. You will close your eyes and finesse the Jack of clubs here, and if you make six, a clear top will probably be yours.

76

Entering the last round of a Regional Open Pairs, you estimate your game is running about 62 or 63 percent. This means that if you can somehow get yourself two complete tops on the last two boards, you will score somewhere around 430 on the session (325 is average), maybe enough for the whole ball of wax despite your mediocre carryover from the Qualifying Session. On the other hand, if you finish with two average-plus results, your score will be about 410, which is the same as oblivion, for all practical purposes. You will finish around ninth or tenth overall, but nobody remembers who finished third, much less tenth.

Your position lends itself to a delightful practice known as "shooting." This means that you will elect to take some rather outrageous chances against your final opponents, hoping to create an unusual result which you hope will be in your favor. Of course, your unorthodoxy may well get you a zero, but that will only mean you will finish twentieth instead of tenth, hardly a consideration if you have your eyes set on first place alone.

Shooting has always been a part of the matchpoint game, but it can give rise to some inequities. If one of your wild shots fails, you may give your *opponents* a top that they don't really deserve, and there is a possibility you could determine the winners of the event all right, but not exactly as you would prefer.

On the first board out, partner finesses for a Queen when missing four cards in the suit (a mildly antipercentage play that the field will avoid). This works out for you and you have your first fine score. Lucky for you that the board provided your side an opportunity to shoot for a top.

This is the second board. You are dealer, looking at:

♠ K4
♡ J5
◇ KQJ863
♣ KQ5

You open ONE DIAMOND and partner responds ONE HEART. RHO now enters wih a DOUBLE. You rebid TWO DIAMONDS, LHO competes with TWO SPADES, and partner goes on to THREE DIAMONDS. Would you take any further action?

■ ■ ■

Sure, you bid THREE NOTRUMP. I know, I know. This is a terrible bid. The trouble is that you have no Aces, a serious deficiency when the opponents clearly have a suit they can set up against three notrump. If you have to knock out lots of Aces, the opponents will probably get the spades established before you can make nine tricks. But if you happen to make three notrump, you will likely have the top score you need to have a chance at winning the event!

All pass to three notrump, with partner giving you a fearful look, as if he knows what you are up to. A low spade is led, and the dummy is really better than you deserve:

♠ 83
♡ AQ62
◇ A5
♣ J10762
□
♠ K4
♡ J5
◇ KQJ863
♣ KQ5

The spade Ace wins on your right and the deuce is returned. If you could only hold up just once! But you have to win, and the situation looks grim. You have only eight tricks, the heart finesse looks certain to lose on the bidding, and you cannot set up clubs without letting the opponents in to run spades against you. You can see how the lack of Aces affects your prospects. If your KQx of clubs were the Axx, you would be cold for three notrump (and your bid would be a lot more reasonable).

Do you see any hope at all to make this?

■ ■ ■

Maybe if you led that Jack of clubs from dummy early, faking a finesse, you could sneak it by the Ace. It would have to be a sleepy RHO who would duck, especially since his partner played a lower spade at trick two than he led at trick one (suggesting more than four cards). But there have been worse plays. How about running all the diamonds? Could that help? RHO could save the club Ace, the guarded King of hearts, and a spade to get to his partner, and have room to spare. No good at all. It looks like the deceptive ploy is your only slim chance.

Hoping to lull RHO, you lead the Queen of diamonds, as if taking a finesse against the King, and a diamond to the Ace. RHO discards a high heart on the second diamond. You are about to call for the club Jack when RHO suddenly says, "Oops, sorry. I have a diamond." You call for the Director (as you always do when there is an infraction of the Laws) instead. The ruling: the low heart is a Penalty Card. Of course, you feel sympathetic toward your chagrined opponent. Think how you would feel if you were in his place. But the most sportsmanlike way to play the game is to take advantage of the Penalty Card if you can. What should you do?

■ ■ ■

In fact, you chose to lead the heart deuce from the table. RHO had to follow with his Penalty Card, and the Jack held for your ninth trick. You got most of the matchpoints for making three notrump and finished second in the event. Nicely done.

It was not until several days later that some sadist pointed out to you that you made the wrong play. You should have gone ahead and led clubs. RHO would win the Ace and would have to *lead* his Penalty Card, allowing you to make the rest, for two overtricks! You demanded to know of partner how much the gaffe had cost in terms of matchpoints. Maybe you could have won the whole thing after all. But luckily for you, he didn't remember.

77

The Principle of Restricted Choice is an elusive and interesting mathematical concept that can be applied to the play of certain suit combinations. Suppose, to use the simplest illustration, that you have Axxx in hand and K109xx in dummy. You choose to cash your Ace, and an honor (either one) falls on your right. It is now correct, in the absence of evidence to the contrary, to *finesse* your LHO for the other honor. The odds in your favor are substantial. *If your RHO had held the doubleton Queen-Jack,* he would have had a choice of equal cards to play from. Presumably, he would play at random; the Queen on some occasions, the Jack on others. Since he did, in fact, play one particular honor, there is a presumption afforded you that he does *not* have the doubleton Queen-Jack, for with that holding, he might equally have played the other honor instead!

Sound like a fantasy to you? Maybe so, but it has a sound mathematical basis. Here's another example. You have Axx opposite dummy's

KQ8x. You play to the King and back to your Ace. RHO follows with the nine and Jack. The odds now favor a finesse of dummy's eight. With J109, your RHO could have played his cards in many different ways at random. But with the doubleton J9, his choice of plays would be much more restricted.

Still sound confusing? OK, here's one more illustration, and this one may be the best. A little guy with a big smile and a green tinted sun visor comes up to you with three pairs of playing cards. One pair consists of two *red* cards, another of two *black* cards, and the third pair, one of *each* color. The pairs of cards are shuffled around and placed face down at random. Then the guy with the cards turns one of them over. It is red. The guy now says he will bet you that the *other* card in this pair is *also* red. Don't bet.

Aside from all this, I can only say one other thing about the Principle of Restricted Choice, and that is ... it works. Often. The Principle has a *great many* applications at bridge. For instance ...

Playing in a cut around Chicago game for only a half cent a point, you are delighted to hold:

♠ AQ
♡ AQ74
♢ KJ5
♣ AQJ10

Your partner is the best player in the group, except yourself, of course, so you may get to make the most of this fine hand. You open TWO CLUBS (playing weak two-bids), and partner responds TWO DIAMONDS, denying a good suit and enough strength to make some positive response. You rebid TWO NO TRUMP, showing a balanced 23-24 HCP, and he carries you to SIX NOTRUMP.

All pass, and the eight of spades is led. You see:

♠ K10
♡ KJ83
♢ A103
♣ 8642
□

♠ AQ
♡ AQ74
♢ KJ5
♣ AQJ10

Partner could have used Stayman, but he did not because he knew your combined high-card strength was more than ample for a notrump slam, and he had little in the way of useful distribution. (Many players would have given a positive response over two clubs with his cards, but apparently, he wanted a longer, stronger suit to respond in a suit, and was unwilling to bid notrump.)

RHO covers dummy's spade ten with the Jack, and you win. You cross to a heart and take the club finesse, which loses. Another spade comes back. You win, and cash your clubs. LHO follows to all four rounds, while RHO pitches spades. Four rounds of hearts come next. This time RHO follows all the way, while one diamond and two spades are discarded on your left. So at this point, you know all about the distribution. LHO was 4-1-4-4, RHO was 5-4-3-1. How should you make your critical diamond guess?

■ ■ ■

There are two indications to point your way. First, LHO had four diamonds, RHO only three. So the odds are four to three that LHO had any particular diamond, including the Queen. The other indication is more subtle, and arises from the Principle of Restricted Choice. If LHO had held four *little diamonds* as well as his four little spades, he might equally have led a diamond against six notrump. He would have had a random choice between two almost identical suits, you see. So your best shot is certainly to finesse LHO for the missing diamond lady.

78

Playing in a "friendly" IMP match (10¢ an IMP, $2 on the match), you pick up:

♠ K7542
♡ Q7
◇ KJ6
♣ 642

With your side vulnerable, your partner opens ONE CLUB. You respond ONE SPADE. He consults the ceiling and raises to TWO SPADES. Should you go on?

■ ■ ■

At IMPs, you have more to gain by bidding a *vulnerable* game with less than an even chance of making than you have to lose if your decision is wrong. (This assumes that, if you are set, it is only by one trick, and you are not doubled. If you're like me, you are *frequently* doubled, so your own personal odds, like mine, may not be so good.) In this case, the decision appears to be very close. If your heart Queen were the Queen of partner's club suit, you would have a clearcut three spade bid. But as it is, the Queen of hearts could lie opposite a doubleton, and your three small clubs look discouraging. You decide to PASS, and two spades becomes the final contract.

LHO leads the Queen of clubs, and you have to struggle to keep your composure when you see dummy. "If you were thinking about bidding again, you'll probably make four," partner says gloomily, as he puts down his hand. Indeed:

♠ AQ94
♡ 83
◇ A7
♣ AJ1095
□
♠ K7542
♡ Q7
◇ KJ6
♣ 642

Maybe if you're lucky, partner won't ever tell you what he was thinking about when he bid only two spades. He has a routine three spade bid, especially vulnerable at IMP scoring. Maybe he had one of his Aces covered up. Anyway, your options at this point are: (1) bawl partner out unmercifully for his idiocy; (2) get up from the table and go commune with the wall for a while; or (3) go ahead and play the hand.

Choosing the latter in order to demonstrate exceptional intestinal fortitude, you win dummy's club Ace and lead a spade to your King. Both opponents follow. Too bad. If RHO had held all four of the missing trumps, your two spade contract would have been a winner. But as it is, four spades will make, and it will surely be bid at the other table. Is there any way at all to extricate yourself from disaster on this hand?

■ ■ ■

Well, actually, no. A big loss in IMPs is inevitable. All you can do is try to make the blow as soft as possible. Draw the rest of the trumps, play a diamond to the Ace, and take the diamond *finesse.* If it works, you will get a heart loser away and make *five,* for plus 200, losing only 9 IMPs when they score up a routine 620 in the replay. This will save your side an IMP (if you are plus only 170, you will lose 450, or *10* IMPs). And the strange diamond finesse cannot cost anything, because if it fails and you make only three, for plus 140, you still lose the same 10 IMPs (480 = 10 IMPs).

Of course, you lost the match by 35 IMPs ($5.50). But you saved a dime, and gained a reputation for character. Not to mention a tenacity unsurpassed in the annals of contract bridge.

79

Your record in the Swiss Teams is 3-0, and dinner would taste a whole lot better if you could eat it undefeated. This is the second hand of your fourth match.

Not vulnerable against vulnerable foes, you pick up:

♠ AJ1094
♡ K109
♢ 93
♣ 1054

Your RHO, the dealer, opens ONE DIAMOND in front of you. Since you adhere strictly to the "sound" approach to simple overcalls, you are not willing to bid one spade here, as most players would do. *Your* overcalls promise more high-card strength and defensive values. But you can take advantage of the vulnerability to make a slightly eccentric weak *jump* overcall. If somebody looks quizzically at your spade length, you can always plead that you had a club in amongst your spades.

All pass to your TWO SPADES, the eight of diamonds is led, and dummy has a lot better support than you usually find there when you make a bid like this:

♠ K863
♡ 74
◇ Q1062
♣ AQ2
□
♠ AJ1094
♡ K109
◇ 93
♣ 1054

RHO wins the Jack of diamonds at trick one, and fires back the Queen of hearts. You cover this, and LHO takes his Ace and returns the five of hearts, taken by RHO's Jack. Now RHO plays the King of diamonds, to which LHO follows with the four, and continues a low diamond. How do you play?

■ ■ ■

You have lost four tricks already, and the danger is that you may lose a trump and, if the club King is wrong, a club as well. (One club loser can be discarded from dummy on your high ten of hearts.)

Assume the worst, that the club King is wrong. *Then RHO is most unlikely to have the spade Queen as well.* Let's "give" RHO some hypothetical hands containing both cards:

♠ Qx
♡ QJx
◇ AKJxx
♣ Kxx

With this one, he would open one notrump, not one diamond.

♠ Q
♡ QJxx
◊ AKJxx
♣ Kxx

With this, he would reopen the bidding over your two spades.

♠ Qx
♡ QJxx
◊ AKJxx
♣ Kx

With this, he would reopen, planning to convert a club response back to diamonds. (Many players would open one notrump with this hand.)

Knowing that, if RHO has the club King, he is most unlikely to have the spade Queen, your proper play is clearly indicated. Ruff the third diamond with the spade Ace, then lead the spade Jack and pass it. If the Queen of spades wins to your right, you can be pretty sure that the club finesse will succeed when you take it later. And you will make your contract exactly.

This hand illustrates what Terence Reese described as a "second-degree assumption." That is, you make an assumption about the location of one card (often assuming the worst), and then you see what conclusions you can draw, based on your assumption.

The ACBL used to run most of its Team-of-Four events on what is called "Board-a-Match" scoring. If you and your partner, for example, played three notrump, making five, and your teammates at the other table found some way to hold three notrump to four in the replay, your team won the board. The team that won the greatest number of boards over one or more sessions of play took the event.

The only problem with Board-a-Match was that it rewarded superior skill so perfectly. The better players won consistently, and the poorer ones could play in Board-a-Match events until they were old and gray without winning even so much as a fraction of a Master Point. The upshot of it all was that the Team events were not particularly well attended.

Perceiving that its need to stay financially solvent and cater to the average player outweighed the duty to provide the most meaningful type of bridge competition, the League introduced Swiss Teams. The tournaments are much larger now, and everybody wins lots of Master Points, but it's a shame, really, that Board-a-Match had to be a sacrificial lamb. It was a great game to play in and a tough one to win. Maybe one of these days, B-a-M will make a strong comeback. But I'm not holding my breath.

Playing Board-a-Match Teams, you pick up:

♠ KQ53
♡ K95
◇ 1093
♣ K98

Nobody is vulnerable. Partner opens ONE DIAMOND and RHO DOUBLES. Your REDOUBLE is passed back to RHO who runs to ONE NOTRUMP. You DOUBLE. Pass; pass; TWO CLUBS by RHO. Without four decent clubs, you can't hit this as well, so you pass to see what partner wants to do. He bids TWO DIAMONDS. You have a close decision to make. Do you raise diamonds, or should you perhaps bid some number of notrump?

■ ■ ■

Your Kings are well placed behind whatever Aces RHO may have, and the opponents don't seem to have a suit they can establish to beat three notrump easily. So you decide to blast aggressively into THREE NOTRUMP. Raising diamonds would be pointless; notrump is the most likely *game,* and *you* are the one with a club stopper.

LHO leads the club deuce, and this is what you see:

♠ J72
♡ A104
◇ AKQ85
♣ 53
□
♠ KQ53
♡ K95
◇ 1093
♣ K98

RHO wins the club Ace and returns the four. This hand doesn't look very exciting, even at Board-a-Match. Clubs seem to be 4–4, so you will knock out the spade Ace, lose three clubs, and claim. Making just three, for a probable half on the board. Can there be anything else to do?

■ ■ ■

Maybe RHO would have trouble discarding on the run of your diamonds. Let's see. Win the third club, and run five diamond tricks. He'll have room for five cards. No, that's no good. He can save a club, the spade Ace, and the QJx of hearts. No problems. If only you had one more diamond ... wait a minute. Just one more winner. If you could sneak a spade past RHO, *then* he might be in trouble when you cash your diamonds. He shouldn't fall for this when you have bid so strongly, but it costs nothing for you to try.

You win the third club, cash the Ace and King of diamonds (sneakily following with your nine and ten), and lead the Jack of spades, faking a finesse against the Queen you hold yourself. RHO ducks and the Jack wins. Now come the rest of the diamonds, the suit having split 3–2. Your RHO begins to look unhappy. As it happens, he holds:

♠ Axx
♡ QJxx
◇ xx
♣ AJxx

On the last diamond, he is stuck. He cannot throw the spade Ace or unguard his hearts, so he discards his last club. Now you can safely knock out the Ace of spades, and lose only three tricks.

If they ever bring back Board-a-Match, you'll be the first one to enter, right?

81

Another form of bridge competition which seems to be regretably near extinction is the Par Contest. There used to be many of these; the National Intercollegiate tournament was run on a Par basis for many years. In a Par competition, the hands are prearranged, and all of them contain one or more points of technique. The players are judged on the basis of how many of these opportunities for good bidding and play they recognize and execute. Maybe the reason Par contests have died out is that all the good "themes" for Par hands were exhausted or overused so that they became too familiar. Nowadays, there are so many fine technicians among the ranks of the bridge players and the standard of play has progressed so far, a typical Par contest might be less of a challenge than it used to be. It would take a real virtuoso to "set" a good series of Par hands today.

Suppose we turn the clock back a few revolutions. This hand is adapted from a Par competition, so you can see how you would have made out in the elder days. As dealer, you hold:

♠ AQ
♡ AQ1094
◇ A32
♣ AJ5

This hand is worth opening, and your options are one heart, two clubs, or two notrump (21–22 HCP). What do you choose?

■ ■ ■

TWO NOTRUMP is your most descriptive bid. You lack the playing tricks to open two clubs and force to game. One heart is not so bad, but with all your tenaces, you want to make sure it is you and not partner who becomes declarer at notrump. Yes, I know that you have a five-card major (horrors!) for your two notrump opening, but you still want to make the bid that best portrays the nature of your whole hand.

Partner raises you to FOUR NOTRUMP. That is not Ace asking, but just a raise of notrump, inviting slam just as a raise of one notrump to two notrump would invite game. Should you accept his invitation?

■ ■ ■

You should accept, since you have a five-card suit and lots of prime values. But you can do so by jumping to SIX HEARTS, giving partner an option. He can always return to notrump if he wants to, but for all you know, his hand might look good for a heart contract. As it happens, partner goes back to SIX NOTRUMP, and all pass.

A heart is led, and this is the dummy you have to work with:

♠ 432
♡ KJ
◇ KJ54
♣ K432
□
♠ AQ
♡ AQ1094
◇ A32
♣ AJ5

How do you plan the play so as to earn your par?

■ ■ ■

You have ten top tricks and all sorts of possibilities for more. There are finesses to take in three suits and the chance of a 3-3 split in either one of the minors. You should prefer to take the *club* finesse to begin with. If you were to take a losing diamond finesse early, a spade return would be awkward. You would have to decide whether to take the spade finesse before you had exhausted all your other options.

Say the club finesse loses and they get out with another heart. You now test clubs to see the break. If clubs are 4-2, you will need the diamond finesse, plus a 3-3 diamond split or the spade finesse. If clubs go 3-3 for you, though, you only need four tricks from diamonds and spades combined, and the best way to get them is to try a combination shot:

Cash the high diamonds, hoping for the Queen to fall; if it does not, fall back on the spade finesse. You get two chances this way instead of just one.

Backtracking a little, suppose that the club finesse *wins* for you at trick two. You would probably go ahead and see if clubs split. If RHO has four or more clubs, you can take the spade finesse safely, reserving the diamond finesse for later if you need it. If LHO turns up with the club length, you can either (1) take the diamond finesse, with the spade finesse, a 3–3 diamond split, or a squeeze in reserve; or (2) you might run your red-suit winners, planning to throw LHO in with the fourth club for a spade return into your tenace.

Since there is a lot of guesswork in the play after a winning club hook, what with the multiple squeeze chances and all, the person who constructed this hand would probably have the club hook lose, so that declarer would have to rely only on his good technique, and not have to guess his way through the rest of the play. That's the idea in any good Par hand.

Some players might run their hearts before taking any finesses. This might prove awkward, mainly because dummy will be squeezed on the fifth heart, and one of declarer's extra chances will be eliminated.

82

Every so often, we hold a Calcutta at my club. Sometimes, this is a Charity affair. The local bridge Association might be in need of a few extra bucks, or one of the bridge players might have fallen on hard times and we help him out. Most often, however, the event is just inspired by some good old fashioned greed. All the pairs in the game are auctioned off. The auction is usually the liveliest part of the evening. You might pay several hundred dollars to buy the chances of a good pair. The proceeds from the auction go into a pot, which is divided among the owners of the top finishing pairs after the game, 40 percent to first place, 25 percent to second, and so on. Any pair may bid on themselves if they want to. And every pair has the option of buying back up to 50 percent of the rights to themselves from whoever bought them.

Playing in a Calcutta (you bought yourself, of course. Sure, nobody else even bid on you, but that just made it like taking candy from a baby), with the stakes just shy of being really scary, you pick up this hand:

♠ A6
♡ J1053
◇ A10752
♣ Q4

You deal and pass, LHO passes, and partner open ONE SPADE in third seat. The opponents do not bid. You respond TWO DIAMONDS. Partner reverses into THREE CLUBS and you make the obvious call of THREE NOTRUMP. Now partner rears back and bids FIVE DIAMONDS. Should you stop here, or go on?

■　■　■

Partner should have excellent diamond support for such a majestic leap to an eleven-trick contract. And he must be interested in slam as well. If his aspirations were limited to game, he could have showed his diamond fit earlier or at a lower level. He would have had no reason to stop off and bid clubs before jumping to the diamond game. In fact, his bidding promises shortness (singleton or, more likely here, void) in the suit he hasn't bid, and invites you to go to slam with a hand that fits well with his. Well, how do you like your hand? You love it? I would too. You have very little waste in hearts (the key feature), reasonable trumps, a couple of Aces, and help in partner's suits. You should bid SIX DIAMONDS, and not be surprised if seven is a make!

All pass to six diamonds, a heart is led, and partner's dummy is very minimum for his bidding:

♠ KJ742
♡ —
◇ KQ63
♣ AJ106
　□
♠ A6
♡ J1053
◇ A10752
♣ Q4

Even with that dog for a dummy, the slam looks like a favorite. If trumps are 2-2, you are cold for it. Otherwise, there will be some work in the play. You ruff the opening lead and cash *one* of dummy's high trumps. If trumps are 4-0, you will need some very good fortune in the black suits. But both opponents follow to a round of trumps. How do you continue?

■ ■ ■

Count some tricks for starters. (Failure to perform this simple operation has led to the downfall of many an easy contract.) Five diamonds, two spades, and three clubs are available. Two heart ruffs in dummy will get us up to twelve. But we need to set up clubs early. Can't risk a losing club finesse when dummy no longer has any trumps, and there are still heart losers in hand.

How about a simple line? Spade to Ace, club finesse. Potential problems. If RHO won, he could return a *club,* putting us in dummy where he could keep an eye on us. We would lack the entries to ruff another heart and get back to hand to draw trumps. (LHO could have the Jxx of trumps and a doubleton spade, and we would get overruffed on the third spade.)

Would it help to try setting up the spades early? Ace, King, and a spade, ruffed low? No guarantees there either. If they overruff the third spade and return a trump, we're short of tricks. Could pitch a club on the third spade instead of ruffing, but then they might beat us by continuing with a fourth spade, promoting a trump trick anyway. Spades isn't the answer. Back to clubs.

A low club from dummy at trick three. Would that work? If the Queen wins(!) or if RHO wins the King, we have an extra entry to hand so that we can ruff another heart and draw trumps. But suppose LHO wins the club King and returns a club. We're back in trouble again, with the same transportation woes. Entries are the whole problem. If we could find an extra entry to hand . . .

How about a spade to the Ace and a *low* club to the Jack? Say it loses, and a club comes back to the Queen. Heart ruff. Still no good. Still stuck in dummy. *Need to preserve the spade Ace.* How about . . . aha! This may be it. The *Jack* of clubs from dummy at trick three. If either opponent wins, you can win the club return in hand, ruff a heart, cash the other high trump in dummy, and get back to the spade Ace to draw any other trump. Now, a spade to the King and the other two clubs. Two hearts go away.

If they duck the club Jack (unlikely, you daresay), you may still have to do a little guessing, but you will be no worse off than if you had adopted some other line of play.

Somebody once stated that if you could take the convoluted thought processes of the expert as his mind ranges over the spectrum of bidding and playing a hand, and show them to an average player, the A.P. wouldn't believe it all.

You made six diamonds, and that helped you to a fourth place finish in the Calcutta. Unfortunately, fourth place money just about reimbursed you for what you paid to buy yourself to start with. So the day was a financial bust instead of the killing you had hoped for. At least, though, you still salvaged enough cash to buy yourself again in the *next* Calcutta.

83

During the bidding, you and partner will customarily try to exchange as much information as possible. Of course, the auction may be summarily cut short if one of you is willing to "bash" into what he thinks is the best spot—sometimes, a brief auction can make the opponents' task on defense somewhat harder—but everyone agrees that whatever early, probing bids you choose to make should be as descriptive as possible.

Playing in a Pairs' event, but with scoring at IMPs, you have:

♠ A94
♡ KJ852
◇ Q93
♣ K5

Nothing to get excited about, but you are willing to open ONE HEART. Partner proceeds to embark on a campaign. He starts with TWO DIAMONDS, and your rebid is TWO NOTRUMP, to show a balanced minimum. THREE CLUBS from partner. You dutifully take a preference to THREE DIAMONDS. Next you hear THREE HEARTS. What should you do now? Diamonds or notrump could still be the right spot, especially if partner's heart support is ragged.

■ ■ ■

You cannot really make an informed decision at this point, so all you can do is pass the buck back over to the other side of the table. Bid THREE SPADES. This is a very eloquent call. Partner can almost hear you speaking to him: "Friend, I have something good in spades, but not so much that I want to insist on notrump. Neither am I anxious to play in hearts opposite three small or a doubleton honor. I am giving you the courtesy of the road. Feel free to bid three notrump with a little help in spades, four hearts if your support is better than I might expect at this time, or, if you want to, four of a minor."

After a modest pause, partner bids THREE NOTRUMP, and you accept this as the contract. The opening lead is the six of spades, and the dummy is promising:

♠ Q2
♡ 743
◇ AK84
♣ AQ103
□
♠ A94
♡ KJ852
◇ Q93
♣ K5

You try the spade Queen from dummy, of course, breathing a silent prayer in the process; and your prayer gets answered this time; the Queen wins, RHO following with the eight.

Since you may need a heart trick, you lead a heart from dummy at the second trick. RHO plays low. What would your guess be?

■ ■ ■

A good opponent might jump up with the Ace here if he had it, to return spades. On the other side of the coin, if you play a confident King, your LHO might duck with Ax! (It might be the correct play from his point of view; he might need to retain his only entry to the spade suit, or he might need to put you to later guess in hearts if your holding were KQ10xx.) There is another slight suggestion that the heart Ace is on your right; some players might overcall one spade over your one heart opening with five decent spades, the heart Ace, and another point or two.

Anyway, having made up your mind, you smoothly play the King from hand. LHO just as smoothly wins the Ace, jolting your confidence somewhat. He leads the two of spades to RHO's Jack. You duck this trick and win the third spade. Where do you go from here?

■ ■ ■

There are many chances remaining to you. Suppose you play off the three top clubs. Both opponents follow, no Jack appears. Next, you try the Ace of diamonds, unblocking the nine, and come to the diamond Queen. Both opponents follow, and the ten is played to your right on the second diamond. A third diamond is led toward dummy and LHO plays low. Do you finesse the eight at this point?

■ ■ ■

The Principle of Restricted Choice suggests you finesse. The mathematical odds are substantially in your favor. But that is the right play only if you are considering the diamond suit in isolation. The right play within the context of this *hand* is the King of diamonds. If RHO's Jack falls, you make at least three. But suppose that RHO shows out. He had two diamonds; and the play suggests that LHO led from a five-card spade suit, leaving RHO with three spades. You know he had four clubs at most, so he had four hearts!

Therefore, you can make three notrump for certain by *winning* the third diamond and leading a heart if RHO cannot follow. RHO will be able to win and cash the club Jack, but he will have to give you a heart in the end.

You could lose the contract by taking a third-round diamond finesse. RHO might win, lead a heart to partner's Queen, and the opponents would take the rest of the tricks. But you can never go wrong by winning the third diamond, not if you trust your count of the opponents' distribution.

84

A little learning is a dangerous thing. Whoever said that must surely have been a bridge player. If you don't think so, read on . . .

The Qualifying Session for the Open Pairs is almost done. You and partner have had a rocky set of boards, the opponents having played over their collective head at your table, and your mood has turned gloomy. You can't afford any boo boos from here on and still hope to qualify. In this precarious situation, you hold:

♠ AKJ73
♡ A5
♢ A742
♣ 86

You open ONE SPADE and partner raises to TWO SPADES. RHO, not vulnerable, comes in with THREE CLUBS. What is your action?

■ ■ ■

At IMPs, you might just bash into game, but at matchpoints, you don't want to be in game unless it is at least a fair proposition. You decide to *try* for game by bidding THREE DIAMONDS. This must show game interest, since you'd pass or bid three spades just to compete otherwise. The three diamond bid will also tell partner that any diamond honors he has will be especially useful to you. If partner has help for you in diamonds as well as spades, then your combined hands fit together well, and you might make game with rather less than 26 points.

Over your three diamonds, partner jumps to FOUR SPADES. All pass to this, and the Queen of clubs is led. Dummy tables:

♠ Q94
♡ 8743
◇ KQ5
♣ 953
□
♠ AKJ73
♡ A5
◇ A742
♣ 86

You see what I mean about "fit"? This contract has a decent chance in spite of your deficient high-card count. RHO overtakes the club Queen and continues with two more high clubs. On the third one, you pitch your losing heart, of course. You cannot afford to ruff high, since trumps could be 4-1, and you will be overruffed if you ruff low. LHO shows out on the third club, and RHO shifts to a heart. You win, and try the Ace and Jack of trumps. Both opponents follow. How do you continue?

■ ■ ■

Of course, you've seen positions like this before. You abandon trumps and try to ruff your fourth diamond in the dummy. This is a no cost play. If somebody has four or more diamonds, you cannot make this hand, unless he or she also has the last trump and has to follow while you ruff your last diamond with dummy's last trump. Of course, if diamonds turn out to be 3-3, you simply draw the last trump and cash your good diamond.

So it can't lose to shift over to diamonds at this point, and it may gain. Right?

■ ■ ■

Wrong. Sorry, but there is a better line. If you tried to ruff your fourth diamond, having seen this theme somewhere before, you were fixed by a *fixation*, a problem that commonly afflicts good players. With RHO known to have eight or nine black cards and LHO only four or five, you should prefer to try squeezing LHO in the red suits. Win a third round of trumps in dummy, and ruff a heart. Go back to dummy with a diamond and ruff another heart. If LHO had four or more diamonds *and* four or more hearts, he will be squeezed at some point, and forced to unguard one of his red suits. (If LHO threw a *heart* from four of them on the third round of clubs, the last heart in dummy will be good now!)

The only time this line of play loses and the other one works is when RHO had 2-4-1-6 pattern, and some players might double two spades with four cards in the other major instead of overcalling. (Your squeeze will also turn up a loser if RHO is 2-5-0-6, but that is impossible on the bidding and the defense.)

Meanwhile, playing for the squeeze will work in a couple of very possible cases (when RHO is 3-3-1-6 or 3-2-2-6) when trying to ruff a diamond in dummy will come to grief.

A little learning is dangerous all right. Remember this hand the next time you start to chastise partner for making a "wrong play."

85

After years and years of subtle effort, you were finally able to lure Eisenberg and Kantar into a set game against you and your favorite partner. Now that you've got them where you want them, don't blow it on this taxing hand.

Vulnerable or not, you hold:

♠ J942
♡ J7642
◇ A7
♣ 53

Partner opens ONE CLUB and you respond ONE HEART, silently giving thanks that it was partner and not the opponents who spoke first. Kantar, to your left, overcalls ONE SPADE, and partner jumps to THREE HEARTS. After a pass on your right, should you consider going on?

■ ■ ■

Well, yes, you should *consider* it. Maybe not for very long, but you should consider it. Seriously, there is a case for a four heart bid. First, you have an extra trump. Your fifth card in hearts is worth as much as a side Queen now that hearts have been jump raised. My experience has been that handling the play with a *nine*-card trump fit as opposed to an eight-card fit is more significant than you might think.

Next, you expect dummy to be *unbalanced*. Partner's sequence promises sixteen to eighteen points in support of hearts; he would open one notrump with a balanced hand in that range. The odds on a singleton spade appearing in dummy are pretty good. Your side card on this hand is an *Ace* (much better than two Queens), that may buy you some time to set up dummy's club suit. You have few wasted values (if your spades were *K*9xx, your hand would not really be much better than it is, with the one spade overcall behind you); and finally, you are *vulnerable,* and the odds on bidding game are much improved.

Inexperienced players sometimes have misconceptions about the implications of vulnerability. You'll hear things like, "I just couldn't bid any more because we were vulnerable." The fact is, you have more to gain than you have to lose by bidding a vulnerable *game,* and so you should be willing to try one even when you think your chances of making are less than even. (See again hand #78.)

Trying not to let your voice quaver, you bid FOUR HEARTS. It comes out a little too loudly, but nobody doubles. The opening lead is the diamond Jack, and when dummy hits, you see that your powers of visualization were on target:

♠ 5
♡ AK105
♢ Q53
♣ AQ962
□
♠ J942
♡ J7642
♢ A7
♣ 53

You cover the Jack of Diamonds hopefully, but dummy's Queen is greeted by the King, and you have to spend your Ace. In spite of that, the vulnerable game still looks like a reasonable undertaking. To make it, you will need either 2-2 trumps (or maybe the singleton Queen and a friendly club division), or the club finesse plus some careful play. Think about how you would proceed. At what point will you draw trumps?

■ ■ ■

Not to begin with. Too much other work to do. It is a sound principle of play that, when the play looks full of problems, your first priority should be to *establish your side suit.* Since you are short of entries to hand anyway, you take the club finesse right away. If it loses, you will need the trump suit to come in, plus some handling. But Eisenberg, on your right, follows with a low club.

Now you can afford *one* high trump. Both opponents follow low. Next, you play the club Ace (the King comes down on your left) and lead a low club. Ten, from your RHO. What should you do?

■ ■ ■

LHO would false card the club King automatically from an original holding of KJx, but you cannot assume he has done this. If you ruff this trick, it might go overruff, spade cash, diamond to RHO, and a fourth club, on which LHO might overruff you again, with the Queen this time. Gruesome. So you pitch your losing diamond on the third club, and Kantar shows out. A diamond is returned, and you ruff. Can you cash another high trump *now?*

■ ■ ■

No. If the trumps were 3-1, you would be made sorry. You could ruff another club to establish dummy's fifth one, but then you would have to lead a spade. The opponents could win and cash their high Queen of trumps, leaving dummy stranded with a diamond loser. To prevent that, you must establish some communication with the dummy by playing a spade now. Eisenberg wins the ten on your right, and pumps dummy with the spade King. *Now* can you play a second trump?

■ ■ ■

'Fraid not. The position is now:

♠ —
♡ K10
◇ 5
♣ 96
□
♠ J9
♡ J76
◇ —
♣ —

Suppose you play the King of hearts, and they show out on your left. You can ruff a club to establish a long card, but when you try to ruff a spade back to dummy to use it, you might be overruffed. You would be stuck with a spade loser in the end.

Instead, you lead dummy's fourth club immediately and ruff with your Jack of hearts, and you are 100 percent safe. If you win this trick, lead to the heart King (at last!), and make four or five depending on the trump position. If they overruff you with the trump Queen, there is nothing they can do to hurt you.

This hand should interest those who like to get the trumps in first and worry about it later. Meanwhile, you briefly, very briefly, entertain thoughts of trying to raise the stakes in the set game.

86

Playing in the last match of a Swiss, you are in contention for all the marbles, as usual. Going into the last deal, you feel like you have slightly the best of it at your table. But needless to say, the bridge gods do not favor you with a flat final board. Instead, you have some delicate decisions to make. Nobody is vulnerable and there are three passes around to you. What should you do with:

♠ AQJ8652
♡ J8
◇ Q7
♣ A10

■ ■ ■

There is a strong temptation to open four spades, counting on partner for a little help, and be done with it. But consider. Both opponents are passed hands, so you won't be preempting anybody (except yourself). You have the ranking suit, so that you can exert some control if the auction does turn competitive. With several side-suit losers, your pattern is wrong for a gambling game bid: four spades could be down easily when you could buy the hand for a makable part score. Finally, you have bits and pieces which could be useful only on defense. If partner has a stiff spade, your only plus score could come from *defending*.

So you open ONE SPADE. Partner responds ONE NOTRUMP. Now what? Should you bid two spades or three spades?

■ ■ ■

This is a very tough guess, since partner could have:

♠ x
♡ Qxx
♢ Kxxx
♣ Qxxxx

and even two spades may go down, or:

♠ 10x
♡ xxx
♢ AJxx
♣ Kxxx

and four spades is a good shot.

You are a little light in high cards for a jump (notwithstanding the seventh spade, which is compensation), and the minor honors in the red suits may not be worth much, so you choose the conservative TWO SPADE rebid. Partner comes up with a raise to THREE SPADES though, and you waste no time in going on to FOUR SPADES.

The club nine is promptly led, and dummy reveals that partner made an imaginative raise (meaning, in the trade, a slightly doubtful raise):

♠ 94
♡ A5
♢ A642
♣ J8743
□
♠ AQJ8652
♡ J8
♢ Q7
♣ A10

Partner knew you had at least six spades, and he obviously fell in love with his Aces and his doubleton heart.

RHO plays the club Queen at trick one. The match (and the event) may be on the line, so plan your play carefully.

■ ■ ■

The club nine looks like a stiff or the top of a doubleton. So crossing to dummy with a red Ace for a finesse in trumps looks very dangerous. Suppose you find LHO with K10x. He wins, puts partner in with whatever red suit you led, they cash a club, and uppercut you with a third round of clubs.

OK, suppose you play Ace and Queen of spades from hand. That might not work either. They could win on your left (holding K10x) and shift to a red suit themselves. You could win, but you would be unable to get off dummy. You might be subjected to the same trump promotion and lose four tricks again.

It seems to be a frustrating hand, since you have plenty of winners if only you could draw trumps. Maybe preserving your communication with dummy is the answer. Suppose you lead the *Jack* of trumps from hand. They win on your right, say, and shift to a red suit. You can draw the rest of the trumps and lead the club ten. They win and cash a red-suit trick, but you will be able to discard your other red-suit loser. If they win on your right and play King and a club immediately, you discard a loser as they ruff on your left, you win the red-suit return, draw trumps, and take your other discard as before.

Is there a snag? Let's be really pessimistic. Suppose they win on your right with the singleton King and return a *low* club for LHO to ruff. Now they shift to a red suit. You win and lead a high club from dummy. They have to duck on your right—if they cover, you ruff high, draw trumps, and claim. So you pitch your red suit loser. They ruff on your left again (with the last outstanding trump this time) and shift to the other red suit. You can win and lead still another club equal. This time they have to cover on your right, else you discard your last red card. So you ruff, and you can get back to dummy with the trump nine for a discard on the last club. There don't appear to be any flaws in your plan, and you do wind up making four.

Leading your Jack of trumps early here leaves a trump in dummy so that you will be able to draw trumps if the opponents threaten you with a red-suit shift. Your precautions are necessary, because the full deal is:

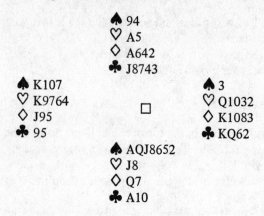

♠ 94
♡ A5
◇ A642
♣ J8743

♠ K107
♡ K9764
◇ J95
♣ 95

□

♠ 3
♡ Q1032
◇ K1083
♣ KQ62

♠ AQJ8652
♡ J8
◇ Q7
♣ A10

The opponents made a spade partial at the other table, and you needed to make this hand to win the match and the Swiss. How did you do?

87

Playing duplicate bridge is one of the best ways to improve your game. A careful study of your results will probably indicate in what areas you're losing points and where you need to study up. Many players have found that the ideal place to carefully study their results is at the local tavern right after the game concludes. The post-mortems often reign long into the night. "What did you do on Board 12?" somebody will ask. And everybody around the table will delve into their Convention Cards and recall whatever gems there were to be had on Board 12.

So here you were with a half-eaten pizza before you, and a large glass of beer. And on this occasion, Board 12 happens to be:

Board 12
West deals
N–S vulnerable

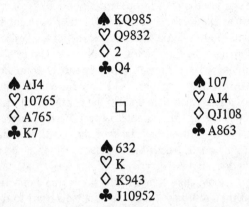

```
                    ♠ KQ985
                    ♡ Q9832
                    ◇ 2
                    ♣ Q4
  ♠ AJ4                          ♠ 107
  ♡ 10765           □            ♡ AJ4
  ◇ A765                         ◇ QJ108
  ♣ K7                           ♣ A863
                    ♠ 632
                    ♡ K
                    ◇ K943
                    ♣ J10952
```

"What did you do on Board 12?" And the tales begin to unfold. One of the sweeter young things said that she had passed as dealer in the West. Her partner opened one diamond in third seat and she responded one heart. There followed three passes, and she managed to make seven tricks, for what proved to be a near zero.

At another table, there was a bit more enterprise. West passed as dealer again, but jumped to two notrump over the third-hand diamond opening instead of bringing forth the ragged hearts. (Responding one heart *as a passed hand* here is questionable; if partner has opened with nothing extra, you may get dropped in one heart, and it could well be a much inferior spot; partner could even have only a doubleton heart.) All passed, and the spade King was led, of course. Declarer won, to insure a second stopper. Unwilling to cross in clubs for a diamond finesse, he led a low diamond from hand. South won and returned a spade, with North ducking to keep communications. Declarer could collect only his eight top tricks, and this too turned out to be worth a mediocre score.

Finally, they asked you what had happened when *you* played Board 12. After all, you had won the duplicate that evening, so your story might be worth a listen. "I was West," you said, assuming a tutorial air, "and I opened ONE DIAMOND. I always hate to pass these decent (2½ Quick Tricks) hands at matchpoints, where making a part-score can conceivably get you a top. Besides, two hands with twelve points opposite twelve will often make a lot of tricks, more than twenty points across from four will produce. With entries in *both* hands, the play is a lot easier to manage."

"Anyway, partner responded TWO CLUBS and I had to rebid TWO NOTRUMP to show a balanced minimum. Partner appreciated the power of his intermediates and went on to THREE NOTRUMP. Notice the significance of our ten-spots, each one of which is potentially useful."

"But you didn't actually *make* three notrump, did you?" somebody asked. "As a matter of fact, I didn't," you replied. "I made *four*. They led the King of spades, and I applied the time honored Grosvenor Gambit* by ducking. It seemed like a good way to break up the opponents' communications, and I figured North would never believe I had ducked with the AJx at the possible cost of a sure trick. Sure enough, he continued spades. He probably thought his partner had the doubleton Jack. I won, crossed to the club Ace, and passed the Queen and Jack of diamonds, winning both times. On the second diamond, North threw a *heart,* which made it look like he had some length in that suit. So my next play was a low heart from dummy. I thought I would play South for a doubleton honor in hearts. The King flew and they returned a spade. I won, led a heart to the Jack, and South pitched a club. So now I knew that North had five hearts, and surely five spades since he did lead that suit against notrump. I cashed my club King, and the Queen had to be a true card when it fell. A heart to dummy's Ace, and South had to throw another club. So I just put him in with his last club, and he had to lead away from his King of diamonds. Easy."

There was a momentary silence up and down the long table, as some people perhaps began to realize why you won the duplicate. A little aggressive bidding and some swashbuckling play are a tough combination to beat. Meanwhile, you helped yourself to another piece of pepperoni, even though it was somebody else's.

---

*An intentional error, but one so patently ridiculous that the opponents cannot believe that it has been made and fail to capitalize. They are, however, dealt a psychological blow because of the missed chance.

88

Your average matchpoint event can be a pretty wild affair. Knowing that a big score will be needed to win, the players, quite a few of them, are right in there swinging from the trees on every possible deal, trying to stir up some action that may lead to a top. Even in the Finals of the National Mens' Pairs, you'll sit down against some mad bulls who are really out to get you. With neither side vulnerable, you hold:

♠ J963
♡ K953
◇ K10753
♣ —

RHO opens ONE CLUB (natural), you pass, LHO responds ONE SPADE, partner passes, RHO raises to TWO SPADES. This is passed around to your partner, who comes to life with a DOUBLE. What are your plans?

■ ■ ■

With partner marked very short in spades, you might be able to take a lot of tricks in either one of the red suits. Even a game is possible; partner could have:

♠ x
♡ AQx
◇ Axxxx
♣ Jxxx

although the opponents would probably still be bidding if he had that hand.

In a case like this, when partner balances, you are usually content to bid a suit cheaply and then subside if the opponents compete further. Your chance of getting a plus score are greater now, thanks to partner's initiative, so you don't punish him by doubling the opponents into game or bidding any more. Here, though, your hand contains features that partner could not have visualized when he balanced (club *void*, no wasted spade honors), so you are justified in competing to at least the *four* level. Your best course (unless you really want to go for the throat and cue-bid three spades) is to bid three hearts now, and then continue with four diamonds if they bid three spades against you. Your partner should expect you to have longer diamonds for this sequence; you would just insist on the major suit if your holding were as long or longer there.

Over your THREE HEARTS, however, LHO DOUBLES. Perhaps you should run to four diamonds, but you decide to stick it out in the nine-trick contract. LHO leads the two of clubs, and this less than ideal dummy hits:

♠ 74
♡ A108
◇ AJ64
♣ QJ73
□
♠ J963
♡ K953
◇ K10753
♣ —

Partner was swinging a bit himself with his balancing double, looking at only three hearts and some wasted club strength. But it's just as easy to get a zero by selling out too cheaply as by going for a "telephone number."

RHO plays the club King on dummy's Queen at trick one. According to the opponents' Convention Card, that two of clubs opening lead is either *third* or *fifth* best. (Many players have adopted this system of opening leads, contending that there are technical advantages over the traditional fourth best approach.)

Plan the play.

■ ■ ■

At first inspection, this looks like a disaster waiting to happen. It's easy to get nervous when playing with such a shaky trump suit, and being doubled in a loud voice doesn't help your composure much. All you can do is try extra hard to keep your wits about you, so that you can put a little added effort into playing the hand well and making the best of the situation as it exists. For instance, don't forget to do your *counting*.

The two of clubs is probably from three cards, since LHO wouldn't double you holding *five* cards in his partner's first bid suit. Spades must be divided 4-3; LHO needed four spades to bid the suit, but RHO couldn't have raised without at least three-card support. How about hearts? LHO surely wouldn't hit you with only two trumps. Could he have four of them? Not likely. Then he would have responded one *heart* to the opening bid, showing his major suits "up the line."

The perilous mists of this hand are clearing for you. LHO must have had 4-3-3-3 pattern. And it's a lot easier to play knowing that. Your best play at this point is to ruff the opening lead and *duck a heart*. Then, if the opponents:

a. play a trump back: win in dummy, ruff another club, and take a first-round diamond finesse to get to dummy to draw the rest of the trumps. Run the diamonds and make three.

b. play a club: Ruff *high*, lead a heart to the ten, and cash the Ace. Pick up the diamonds, playing LHO for three cards.

c. tap the dummy with three rounds of spades: accept the tap, cash the heart Ace, come to the diamond King, draw trumps, and finesse in diamonds.

d. return a diamond (!): win dummy's Jack (or Ace, if necessary). You will have to ruff a club high, and lead a heart, finessing dummy's ten to get the entry to dummy you need to draw trumps.

The opponents' hands are:

♠ A1085		♠ KQ2
♡ Q74		♡ J62
♢ Q92	□	♢ 8
♣ 862		♣ AK10954

You can see that, with your side not vulnerable, your LHO's double was strictly from Limburger. But he might get away with it unless you play your very best.

89

Playing in a one session Board-a-Match tune up the night before the Vanderbilt starts, you encounter a tactical problem:

♠ K5
♡ 6
◇ AKQ4
♣ AJ8542

You are vulnerable, they aren't. You hold this hand in second seat, and after a pass on your right, you open ONE CLUB. LHO considers and bids TWO CLUBS. RHO alerts you that this is conventional, and upon inquiry, you learn that they play the bid to show a weakish hand with length in both major suits.

It used to be that a direct cue-bid of opener's suit showed a hand you would have opened with a forcing two bid. But the opportunity to use a direct cue-bid like that only came up once in a lifetime, so people devised more practical ways to treat a direct cue-bid. The variation your opponents are using is called "Michaels."

Over two clubs, your partner says DOUBLE, indicating that he thinks your side has the majority of the high card strength. RHO dutifully pulls to TWO HEARTS, and you try THREE DIAMONDS. Now LHO jams the auction with a leap to FOUR HEARTS. Partner raises to FIVE DIAMONDS, and RHO goes on to FIVE HEARTS. That leaves you with a tough decision to make. What are your thoughts?

■ ■ ■

Your chances in six diamonds surely must be excellent, even allowing for the probability of bad breaks. To bid the eleven-trick game with the bad trumps you know he has, partner must be looking at some prime cards, like a major suit Ace and the club King. But even assuming you can make six diamonds, will the opponents let you play it? It sounds like they would be inclined to save, especially if you bid a confident sounding six right now. Your best course may be to jockey for position. You can pass five hearts around as though you are uncertain what to do.

(But it is unethical to think for a long time merely for the opponents' benefit, or emit some plaintive moans and groans.) If partner doubles, as he will probably do with his shaky trumps, you can pull to six diamonds, and the chances of your being left alone may improve. Very good opponents might sense what you are up to, but most opponents will not be sure. Of course, partner may bid, but you will be no worse off if he does.

Everything goes as you plan. You PASS, partner DOUBLES, and you pull to SIX DIAMONDS. Then everyone passes, not without some contemplation by the opponents. The heart Queen is led, and partner puts down a minimum dummy:

♠ Q963
♡ A5
◇ J972
♣ K73
□
♠ K5
♡ 6
◇ AKQ4
♣ AJ8542

You may or may not have made a good guess in letting yourself be pushed into six diamonds. Plan the play.

■ ■ ■

You win the heart Ace, and ruff dummy's low heart right away. If diamonds go 4-1, as they quite possibly will, you need to take your ruff now, being short of entries to dummy. Next, you play off the Ace and King of diamonds. If both opponents follow, LHO is quite likely to be void in clubs. In that case, you cannot draw the last trump, because you will need it as a later entry to the club suit. Also, you will need a spade trick to come to twelve altogether, and you cannot wait until all your trumps are exhausted to try to get it. Your best play would be a low spade away from your King. If LHO ducks, you switch to clubs. You cannot make the hand if LHO has the last trump and is void in clubs.

What actually happened, however, was that LHO showed out on the second trump. You continued with your diamond Queen, crossed to dummy with the club King (as LHO played the nine), and drew the last trump with dummy's Jack. Then you took a deep breath and led a club back toward your hand. Ten, on your right. This will be embarrassing if you misguess. You will be down about six. Does LHO have a stiff club as well as a stiff diamond?

■ ■ ■

There are some indications that may or may not be valid. RHO might have jumped preemptively in hearts over the double of two clubs at this vulnerability if he had as many as five cards in the suit. And LHO did take an unusual bid; he leaped to four hearts, which he might not have done with a normal type hand with 5-5 in the majors. Also, the opponents' decision not to save suggests that somebody thinks they might have a trick to beat you with. This is more likely to be Q10x on your right than Qx on your left.

After as much thought as time allows, you decide to finesse. All is well, as LHO discards. You lose a spade in the end, and make six diamonds. LHO was 5-6-1-1, as you guessed.

If you had known six diamonds would be such a headache, you might have stood for the double of five hearts. Actually, you needed to bid to win the board. Your teammates at the other table saved at six hearts over six diamonds, and went for 500, losing a trick in each suit.

90

In the midst of writing this book, I went to the Spring National tournament. I always try not to miss the Nationals (which are held three times a year), because of the excitement the Championship events generate, and because I get to renew many of my old acquaintances. Everybody who is anybody in the bridge world is there.

Some people can't get so excited about attending a Nationals. It's true that the crowds are usually huge and you can get trampled underfoot at worst, and at best you are made to feel small and insignificant in the middle of an endless sea of bridge players. But to me, it always seems like the only place to be. And nowhere is the action more frenetic than just outside the playing area where the Vanderbilt Knockout Teams, the premier event of the tournament, is held.

As the hour grows late and each match nears its completion, the crowds begin to gather and wait expectantly for the results. How does Precision stand? How are the Aces doing? They were down 15 at the half but ... The babble is deafening. Then, from time to time, the players begin to emerge from the Closed Room into this seething mass of solid people, the tension plainly visible on their faces, and rush to where their teammates wait anxiously to compare the results. A thick phalanx of people surrounds them, peering intently over their shoulders while they go down the Card, down the row of numbers, noting a welcome gain here, debiting a fearful loss there, all the while keeping a fateful running total so they will know instantly whether the match has been won or lost after 64 tough boards. Then comes a moment like no other I know of, filled with despair or elation, one of the two. This is the essence of the intensely competitive world of tournament bridge.

You went into the last quarter of the match up by 5 IMPs, which is little better than being tied. One slip could mean that you will not play in the Vanderbilt again tomorrow. Early in the quarter, you pick up:

♠ A4
♡ AKJ752
◇ 106
♣ 752

You open ONE HEART and partner responds ONE SPADE. You rebid TWO HEARTS, and he thinks for a long time and puts it into FOUR HEARTS. While you are wondering what took partner so long to bid, LHO leads the seven of diamonds. Apologizing for his support, partner first displays two small hearts. Obviously, the cause of the delay. The rest of his hand, thankfully, is not so bad:

♠ KJ1072
♡ 63
◇ AQ5
♣ A94
□
♠ A4
♡ AKJ752
◇ 106
♣ 752

Partner really doesn't have to apologize for raising you with two "grunts," because your two heart rebid suggested at least a six-card suit. With only five hearts, you would always have had another option: either a second suit to bid, a spade raise, or a rebid of one notrump. Clearly, partner could have jumped to three notrump instead of raising hearts, but he was probably afraid to with no tenace holding in clubs. He feared you might have a hand like:

♠ Ax
♡ KQJxxx
♢ Kxx
♣ xx

Perhaps partner shouldn't have masterminded by trying to figure out what your hand was, instead of just bidding what was in front of his nose. But that's all in the past now. All you have to do is find a way to make four hearts. How do you choose to play it?

■ ■ ■

You retreated into a strange intuitive world where possible lines of play, like bolts of lightning on a stormy night, flickered and died rejected. No line stood out like a beacon to point your way. After four minutes you gave up on inspiration and relied strictly on instinct. And you did it. You found the best line. You flew with the diamond Ace, cashed both of your high trumps, as the opponents followed low. Then you played the spade Ace, a spade to the King, and led the spade Jack. RHO played low, and you discarded your diamond loser. LHO ruffed with his trump Queen, and you were safe. You made all six of your hearts in hand, two spades, and the two minor-suit Aces.

Much later that night, when the euphoria of winning had made a slight retreat, you found out that your opposite number in the other room had decided on a different approach. He finessed the diamond Queen at trick one. The King won, and your teammates took the opportunity to shift to clubs. Declarer cashed the high trumps, and played spades in the same fashion you did, but your defender *covered* the third spade with his Queen. Declarer had no counter, and went down a trick. The full deal was:

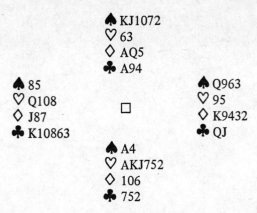

♠ KJ1072
♡ 63
◇ AQ5
♣ A94

♠ 85
♡ Q108
◇ J87
♣ K10863

♠ Q963
♡ 95
◇ K9432
♣ QJ

♠ A4
♡ AKJ752
◇ 106
♣ 752

The declarer at the other table could have succeeded by ducking the diamond lead completely and giving up on the trump finesse later (to avoid exposing himself to a trump promotion). But no line is as good as the one you chose. Whether you found the best play be luck or skill is a moot question. The bottom line is that you bought yourself another day in the pressure cooker again tomorrow. You may need to be instinctive again.

part four

EPILOGUE

After fifteen years of trying to locate the Golden Key to this lovely game, I have one complaint about it and one only.

You learn to play bridge, you become fascinated by it, then engrossed with it. It can easily get to be an obsession. You become a student of the game, a dedicated peruser of all the textbooks, both elementary and advanced, you can get your hands on. You learn all about the fine points, the coups, the abstruse squeezes, the magnificent deceptive plays. You launch out into the world of bridge armed to the teeth with all the fearsome weapons of the expert's repertoire, intimately familiar with all those things that make this game unique and special and exquisite and revered.

And the real world of bridge turns out to be a disillusionment. You win. But you win, not by filling the skies with brilliant and imaginative plays conjured up on the spur of the moment, but by guessing, just guessing, whether to play a King or a Jack. You win by playing two clubs when the opponents are cold for four spades, or when they forget to double you in your save. You win by watching somebody go down in a game so cold that icicles seem to hang from the cards. You make fewer egregious errors than the other guy, and you win. You get lucky, and you win. Maybe a finesse works for you. If the next one loses, you lose along with it. Life can be a finesse.

It is a hard blow to the altruist in you, who waits impatiently for the chance, just a chance, to pull off one of those beautifully devastating plays that the textbooks are always trumpeting. You keep looking for the chance, but your smother play just never seems to come calling.

About five years ago I had a chance to execute a trump coup. It was at the Nationals in Atlanta. The Life Masters Mens' Pairs. And I blew it. I slightly mistimed the play, and in the end I was marooned in the wrong hand. My coup faded and died unborn. No doubt fate will contrive to punish me by withholding another such opportunity until I'm too old and senile to see it, much less do anything about it.

Now, one thing I'm morally certain of is that if I'm ever West in this layout,

```
            Qxxxx
K J10        □             xxx
            Ax
```

and they're in one notrump against me, I will *unhesitatingly* drop my King when declarer lays down his Ace. But will the moment ever come?

I've searched my brain diligently, and I can remember just once bringing off what might be called a "textbook" type play. I'll give it to you as a problem, which you will no doubt solve with alacrity if you are a bookworm:

```
♠ 1094
♡ 7
♢ Q10752
♣ K753
   □
♠ Q6
♡ KJ53
♢ AJ94
♣ AQ2
```

You open ONE NOTRUMP on the South cards, and all pass. LHO leads the six of hearts, and RHO furnishes the ten. What do you do?

■ ■ ■

Right. You win the *King* of hearts, cross to the club King, and take the diamond finesse. It loses, but now LHO thinks that his partner has the heart Jack, and underleads (or cashes) his high hearts instead of switching to spades. You wind up making three or four instead of going down a couple, thanks to your false card at trick one.

I actually made this play. I made it and it worked! It was one of the high points of my bridge playing career. Even after the opponents started some silly argument about whose fault the defense was, I was still tickled pink and my heart pounded with pleasure. This was really what the game was all about. And I had passed the test!

Sadly, I think I've not made another "textbook" play since. Maybe they should rewrite all the textbooks and devote more space to the factors that really determine who wins at bridge. Or perhaps I should get out and play more instead of tapping away at my typewriter. I really should give fate a chance, I suppose.

Glossary

ACBL. The American Contract Bridge League, the organization that sponsors and franchises most of the tournament bridge played in North America.

Board-a-match. A type of scoring used in Team competition, in which one point is awarded for winning each hand (by any margin), and one-half point for tying it.

Club duplicate. A duplicate game, run locally by one of the approximately 5000 clubs affiliated with the ACBL.

Convention card. A printed card through which you and your partner fulfill the obligation to make known what methods you have agreed to use in the auction and in defensive card play.

Gold points. Master Points awarded for overall placings and section tops in Regional and National competition. A certain number of these are required to achieve Life Master ranking.

IMPs. International Match Points, a type of scoring used in Team competition. The difference in *total points* scored on each hand is converted to IMPs according to a scale established by the World Bridge Federation. If, for example, your team wins 50 points at one table and 420 at the other, your total gain is 470, which, on the scale, converts to 10 IMPs.

Knockout teams. A team event with brackets and seeding, in which the winner of each match advances to the next round, and the loser is eliminated.

Life Master. A player who has 300 or more registered Master Points, of which 50 must be *Red* and 25 *Gold.*

Matchpoints. The type of scoring used in duplicate competition among pairs, in which several results are compared.

National tournament. Run three times a year by the ACBL, these last ten days and attract thousands of players. Several National Championships are decided at each one.

Red points. Master Points won in National or Regional competition. A quantity of these are required for Life Master ranking.

Regional tournament. A large tournament, usually lasting several days, sponsored by one of the ACBL's twenty-five Districts.

Sectional tournament. A tournament, frequently held over a weekend, sponsored by one of the League's over three hundred Units.

Swiss Teams. A Team event in which the contestants play a series of short matches. Pairings are determined by pitting teams with similar won-lost records.

Team-of-four. A type of competition in which two pairs play as team-mates, seated at different tables and in opposite directions. Identical hands are played at each table, allowing the usual comparison of results.

For those interested in the world of tournament bridge, further information and materials may be obtained (free for the asking) from:

ACBL
2200 Democrat Road
P.O. Box 161192
Memphis, Tennessee 38116

Index